LUXEMBOURG TRAVEL GUIDE 2023

"Experience the Grand Duchy of Luxembourg: A World of Culture, Cuisine, and Natural Beauty"

BY

JOAN A. PEARL

All rights reserved. No part of this publication may be reproduced, distributed, or transmitted in any form or by any means, including photocopying, recording, or other electronic or mechanical methods, without the prior written permission of the publisher, except in the case of brief quotations embodied in critical reviews and certain other noncommercial uses permitted by copyright law. Copyright © 2023 by Joan A. Pearl.

TABLE OF CONTENTS

Welcome to Luxembourg 6

CHAPTER ONE 10

    WHAT TO KNOW BEFORE PLANNING YOUR TRIP 10

    HISTORY OF LUXEMBOURG 12

    CULTURE AND TRADITION OF LUXEMBOURG 14

    CLIMATE AND GEOGRAPHY 23

    LANGUAGE AND RELIGION 27

    CULTURAL ETIQUETTE 32

    DINING ETIQUETTE 36

    TRAVEL REQUIREMENTS 40

    TRAVEL RESTRICTIONS 47

    UNDERSTANDING FOREIGN CURRENCY AND TRANSACTIONS 51

    CONSIDERING USING SIM OR WIFI IN LUXEMBOURG 57

    VACCINATION NEEDED 66

CHAPTER TWO 71

GETTING TO LUXEMBOURG 71
WHEN TO VISIT LUXEMBOURG 80
WHERE TO STAY IN LUXEMBOURG 87
LUXURY ACCOMMODATION 90
FRIENDLY BUDGET 114
WHAT TO DO IN LUXEMBOURG 151
WHAT TO PACK TO LUXEMBOURG
.... 158

CHAPTER THREE 173
   FOODS AND DRINKS 173
   RESTAURANTS 176
   BARS AND PUBS 181

CHAPTER FOUR 188
   SHOPPING AND MALL 188
   MARKET IN LUXEMBOURG 194
   SHOPPING DISTRICTS IN LUXEMBOURG 199

CHAPTER FIVE 208
   ENTERTAINMENT 208
   NIGHTLIFE 213

MUSIC 218
FESTIVAL 227
CHAPTER SIX 237
   GETTING AROUND 237
   PUBLIC TRANSIT 245
   TAXIS 253
CHAPTER SEVEN 258
   THE DOS AND DONTS OF A TOURIST
   258
   HEALTHY AND SAFETY TIPS 263
   GENERAL TIPS 269
   CONSIDERABLE SAVING TIPS 273
CHAPTER EIGHT 278
   RESOURCES 278
   FUN FACTS ABOUT LUXEMBOURG 286
   SUMMARY 291

Welcome to Luxembourg

I recently had the privilege of traveling to Luxembourg, and the beauty of this tiny nation completely astounded me.

In Luxembourg City, the nation's capital, I began my journey. The city boasts a distinctive blend of old and new buildings, and I was astounded by the breathtaking views of the Old Town from the top of the Bock Promontory. I spent some time wandering the cobblestone streets, marveling at the stunning architecture, and discovering the fascinating history of the place. I also went to other well-known sites, such as the Casemates du Bock, Notre Dame Cathedral, and the Grand Ducal Palace.

From there, I traveled into the countryside and was astounded by how beautiful this tiny nation's environment was. I went to the Mullerthal Region, which is referred to be Luxembourg's "Little Switzerland." As I trekked through the dense woodlands, I marveled at the breathtaking vistas of the area's undulating hills, sparkling streams, and charming villages. I also went to the Vianden Castle, which is one of Europe's best-preserved castles and dates back to the 11th century.

On my final day, I went to Diekirch, the northern region's capital. An outstanding battle memorial honors the American soldiers who took part in the Battle of the Bulge during World War II in this area. I also went to Echternach, a small town famous for the "Echternach Jump," a traditional dance. It was a complete dream for me to visit Luxembourg. The nation boasts breathtaking natural beauty, incredible architecture, and lengthy history. Anyone searching for a unique vacation should visit this magnificent nation!

Being a tourist in Luxembourg was an incredible experience for me. The country's stunning scenery, from the Mullerthal Region's thick woods to the outlying areas' undulating hills, astounded me. I also went to several of the well-known sites in the nation, like the Casemates du Bock, Notre Dame Cathedral, and the Grand Ducal Palace. I also had the chance to learn about the country's rich history and culture, which included the Echternach folk dances and the Diekirch war memorial. I loved getting to know the kind inhabitants and had a great time traveling about this tiny but intriguing nation.

CHAPTER ONE

WHAT TO KNOW BEFORE PLANNING YOUR TRIP?

Being a tourist and organizing a vacation to Luxembourg may be thrilling and rewarding. But before you go on your vacation, it's crucial to make sure you know what to anticipate, what to pack, and how to best organize your trip.

It's crucial to first get acquainted with Luxembourg's culture and traditions. Despite being a very tiny nation, Luxembourg has a rich cultural background, so understanding it might help you get the most out of your trip. It's also crucial to familiarize yourself with Luxembourg's current rules, laws, and expectations if you want to remain in the nation for a lengthy amount of time or are intending to do business there.

Second, you need to look at Luxembourg's top tourist attractions. The magnificent Moselle Valley, the Ardennes Mountains, and the ancient metropolis of Luxembourg City are just a few of the extraordinary experiences and locations in Luxembourg. Plan your schedule, keeping in mind the different sights and things to do that Luxembourg has to offer.

Finally, it's crucial to think about the logistical elements of your journey. Before you go, be careful to set up the required visas and paperwork, choose your travel and lodging alternatives, and create a budget. Researching the different safety measures, you should take while in Luxembourg, such as avoiding travel to risky places and abiding by local regulations, is also a smart idea.

The best way to experience a distinctive culture and see some of Luxembourg's most stunning attractions is to plan a vacation there. Plan and do your homework to make sure your vacation runs as well as possible. You may get the most out of your trip to this intriguing nation with a little planning.

HISTORY OF LUXEMBOURG

A tiny nation in western Europe, Luxembourg has a long and intriguing history. Count Siegfried of Ardennes, the man who started the House of Luxembourg, founded it in 963. The province would be ruled by his line for many decades until Maria Theresa, the final monarch, passed away in 1814.

During the Middle Ages, the House of Luxembourg was one of the most influential families in Europe, and its kings had a significant influence on the formation of the Holy Roman Empire. The area was a significant hub for commerce and manufacturing at the time, and its monarchs were well-known for their support of the humanities.

Following its annexation by France in 1795, the nation went through a time of political unrest during the Napoleonic Wars. Luxembourg joined the German Confederation after the Treaty of Paris in 1815, and it was given its constitution in 1841. The German Confederation was dissolved in 1867, and Luxembourg gained independence.

As a key military hub during World War I, Luxembourg had a significant impact. German troops ruled it throughout both World Wars, and from 1944 to 1945, it was under Allied rule. It was designated a neutral state in 1945, and it joined the European Union in 1948.

Luxembourg is a member of the European Union today and an affluent, secure nation. It is well known for its robust economy, moderate tax burden, and excellent level of life. Additionally, the nation is also known for its stunning landscapes, castles, and museums, which attract tourists from all over the globe.

It is impossible to exaggerate Luxembourg's significance to Europe given its lengthy and varied history. The history of Luxembourg, from its inception in 963 to its present-day position as a successful and stable nation, is a monument to the tenacity and fortitude of its people.

CULTURE AND TRADITION OF LUXEMBOURG

A tiny nation in western Europe, Luxembourg has a long and intriguing history. Count Siegfried of Ardennes, the man who started the House of Luxembourg, founded it in 963. The province would be ruled by his line for many decades until Maria Theresa, the final monarch, passed away in 1814.

During the Middle Ages, the House of Luxembourg was one of the most influential families in Europe, and its kings had a significant influence on the formation of the Holy Roman Empire. The area was a significant hub for commerce and manufacturing at the time, and its monarchs were well-known for their support of the humanities.

Following its annexation by France in 1795, the nation went through a time of political unrest during the Napoleonic Wars. Luxembourg joined the German Confederation after the Treaty of Paris in 1815, and it was given its constitution in 1841. The German Confederation was dissolved in 1867, and Luxembourg gained independence.

As a key military hub during World War I, Luxembourg had a significant impact. German troops ruled it throughout both World Wars, and from 1944 to 1945, it was under Allied rule. It was designated a neutral state in 1945, and it joined the European Union in 1948.

Luxembourg is a member of the European Union today and an affluent, secure nation. It is well known for its robust economy, moderate tax burden, and excellent level of life. Additionally, the nation is also known for its stunning landscapes, castles, and museums, which attract tourists from all over the globe.

It is impossible to exaggerate Luxembourg's significance to Europe given its lengthy and varied history. The history of Luxembourg, from its inception in 963 to its present-day position as a successful and stable nation, is a monument to the tenacity and fortitude of its people.

A wide range of traditions and customs are practiced in Luxembourg. Along with the more contemporary traditions and practices of the twenty-first century, they include national folk music, dancing, and clothes. Both residents and visitors like attending music events like the Rock a Field Festival and the Luxembourg Music Festival. Numerous cultural occasions and festivals are also held, including the Luxembourg Open Air Music Festival and the Luxembourg City Film Festival.

A significant component of Luxembourg's culture and identity is its customs and traditions. The customs and traditions of Luxembourg are a source of pride for its residents and a source of attraction for tourists from all over the globe, from its old folk music and dances to its contemporary festivals and events.

A tiny nation in western Europe, Luxembourg has a vibrant and varied culture. Its history and the influences of its neighbors, like France, Germany, and Belgium, have formed its customs and traditions.

Numerous classic holidays, including Christmas and Easter, as well as contemporary holidays, like Valentine's Day and Halloween, are observed throughout the nation. Good Friday, National Day, and Carnival are a few other traditional celebrations.

The cuisine of Luxembourg is diverse and well-known dishes include kniddelen (dumplings) and Judd mat gaardebounen (smoked pig and broad beans). The quetschentaart (plum tart) and the gromperekichelcher are examples of traditional pastries and sweets (potato pancakes).

In Luxembourg, music has a significant role in culture. Schlager, polka, and waltz are examples of traditional music, although more contemporary genres like rock and hip-hop are also well-liked.

Football, basketball, cycling, and tennis are some of the most well-liked sports in Luxembourg. One of the most significant occasions in the nation is the yearly Tour de Luxembourg bicycle race.

With several fashion designers and businesses established there, Luxembourg is as well renowned for its fashion industry. Both casual and luxury attire are in vogue.

The traditions and customs of Luxembourg are a significant component of its culture, and both residents and tourists appreciate them. Everyone may find something to enjoy in Luxembourg, from contemporary sports and fashion to traditional festivals and foods.

As a visitor, I had a wonderful time experiencing Luxembourg's culture and traditions. I got to experience the country's numerous features, from its historical buildings and castles to its present-day festivals and activities.

My trip's visit to the Luxembourg City Film Festival was one of its highlights. In addition to meeting some of the producers and stars, I got the opportunity to view some of the finest movies ever made. I will always remember it as an incredible experience.

I also got the chance to see some of the most stunning castles and historic locations in the nation. I had the opportunity to learn about the rich history and culture of the nation, from the magnificent Castle of Vianden to the Grand Ducal Palace in Luxembourg City.

It was also incredible to experience Luxembourg's traditional music and dancing. I was able to hear some of the more contemporary musical styles as well as see the schlager, polka, and waltz played live.

I finally got a chance to experience some of the nation's delectable food. I was able to sample the many tastes of Luxembourg, from the traditional Judd of gaardebounen (smoked pork and broad beans) and kniddelen (dumplings) to the more contemporary fare.

I had an amazing time seeing Luxembourg's culture and traditions as a visitor overall. I got the opportunity to discover the numerous elements of this lovely nation, from its ancient buildings and castles to its traditional music and food.

CLIMATE AND GEOGRAPHY

Located in the center of Western Europe, the small nation of Luxembourg is bordered by France, Belgium, and Germany. The nation is renowned for its verdant, lush landscape and temperate climate, which features warm summers and mild winters.

Rolling hills, dense forests, and a variety of waterways, including lakes and rivers, define Luxembourg's landscape. The greatest river is the Moselle, which marks the boundary with Germany, and is supplied by several tributaries, including the Sûre and Our.

Luxembourg's location in the center of Western Europe moderates its climate. With average summertime temperatures in the mid to upper 20s Celsius (roughly 79°F), the summers are hot and muggy. Winters are moderate, with temperatures ranging from 0°C (32°F) to 12°C (54°F). An average of 700 mm of precipitation falls throughout the year, fairly evenly distributed.

Luxembourg's geography is also quite varied. The northern section of the nation is primarily flat and low-lying, whereas the southern part is marked by high hills and valleys. The Kneiff, at an elevation of 560 meters, is the highest point in the nation (1,837 feet).

Luxembourg is home to a variety of animal species, including wild boar, deer, badgers, foxes, and numerous birds, as well as a variety of amphibians and reptiles. The country is also home to a variety of protected places, notably the Upper Sûre Nature Park, which is a wetland region of worldwide significance.

With its undulating hills, luxuriant forests, and a wide variety of wildlife, Luxembourg is an attractive nation. The nation is also renowned for its temperate climate, which makes it the ideal vacation spot for those seeking a relaxing getaway.

As a visitor, I had the pleasure of visiting Luxembourg, and I was astounded by its beauty. My journey was made possible by the ideal weather, which included warm summers, moderate winters, and plenty of sunlight. Beautiful undulating hills, dense woods, and many streams make up the scenery. The variety of fauna, which included wild boar as well as deer, badgers, and foxes, also astounded me. Highlights were the Upper Sûre Nature Park, where I delighted in exploring the wetlands and discovering the value of conservation. I had a favorable overall experience with Luxembourg's environment and temperature, and I would suggest a trip to anybody seeking a tranquil vacation.

LANGUAGE AND RELIGION

One of the smaller nations in Europe, Luxembourg is very diverse in terms of language and culture. French and German are also commonly spoken, but Luxembourgish, a Germanic language related to German and Dutch, is the official language. Furthermore, Luxembourg is a religiously diverse country, having a sizable minority of Protestants and Muslims in addition to a sizable Roman Catholic majority.

The official language of Luxembourg, Luxembourgish, is at the core of its culture. Luxembourgish has its unique personality while being connected to German and Dutch. Although it is mostly spoken in Luxembourg, it is also found in certain areas of Belgium, France, and Germany. The German alphabet serves as the foundation for Luxembourgish's written language, which also uses certain French, Dutch, and English terms. Because of the distinctive blending of elements, it is challenging to learn yet rewarding for those who put in the effort.

Since the days of the Holy Roman Empire, the Roman Catholic Church has had a significant role in shaping Luxembourg's culture. With almost 70% of the people identifying as Catholic, Catholicism is the most prevalent religion in Luxembourg. Luxembourg's culture and politics have been greatly influenced by the Roman Catholic Church, especially in the area of education.

Around 20% of the inhabitants in Luxembourg identify as Protestant, making it the second most common religion. Luxembourg's language and culture are connected with Protestantism, which has a long history there. Compared to other regions of Europe, Protestant churches in Luxembourg often have a more conservative stance.

The third most practiced religion in Luxembourg is Islam. There are several mosques and Islamic institutions all around the nation, and about 5% of the population considers themselves Muslims. Despite a few instances of intolerance and xenophobia, Muslims in Luxembourg have usually been effectively incorporated into society.

With a diverse mix of languages and faiths, Luxembourg is an exceptional country. A culture that is both varied and exciting has been produced as a result of the interaction of all these many influences. There is plenty to discover and enjoy for everyone in Luxembourg, regardless of one's interest in the country's history, religion, or language.

COMMON SENTENCE A TOURIST IN LUXEMBOURG SHOULD LEARN.

Gëff ech Iech eng Hand - Let me shake your hand.

Salut, wéi geet et dir? - Hi, how are you?

Ech verstinn keng Lëtzebuergesch - I don't understand Luxembourgish.

Merci villmools - Thank you very much.

Kënnt Dir mir hëllefen? - Can you help me?

Wou ass d'Toilett? - Where is the bathroom?

Villmools Merci fir Är Hëllef - Thank you very much for your help.

Ech sinn op der Sich no ... - I am looking for...

Kann ech eppes bestellen? - Can I order something?

Wéini ass d'Schlusszäit? - What is the closing time?

Kann ech ee Taxi kréien? - Can I get a taxi?

Kann ech e bësse Lëtzebuergesch schwätzen? - Can I speak a little Luxembourgish?

CULTURAL ETIQUETTE

Travelers and tourists should show respect for Luxembourg's distinctive and frequently complex cultural etiquette. Visitors should be informed of the subtleties of Luxembourg's culture before arriving as the country's lengthy history and reputation as a multicultural nation have a significant impact on cultural etiquette.

The use of language is one of the most crucial components of Luxembourg etiquette. Luxembourgers prefer to speak their native tongue as often as possible since they are proud of it. Before traveling to Luxembourg, visitors should take an effort to learn at least a few fundamental phrases because it will show that they appreciate the local way of life. The nation's three official languages are French, German, and

Luxembourgish, which is very significant to note. Different languages are more often spoken in different regions, thus it's crucial to pick the right one while speaking with natives.

Luxembourgers frequently shake hands when they greet one another, but they can also give each other a hug or a kiss on the cheek. It's crucial to keep in mind that the right greeting should be used depending on the locale and the individuals you are meeting. Visitors should also be aware that it could take some time for Luxembourgers to become used to meeting new people and feel comfortable with a new face.

Keeping in mind that Luxembourg is a Catholic nation and that visitors should respect local religious traditions is especially vital. This involves refraining from discussing religion, dressing modestly, and avoiding public shows of affection.

Finally, guests should be kind and considerate, as Luxembourgers typically are. This entails being polite, speaking at a low volume, and abstaining from using foul words. Additionally, it's crucial to keep in mind to be patient and understanding when interacting with locals as well as to remember to say "please" and "thank you" when it's appropriate.

Overall, Luxembourg's cultural etiquette is rather complex, therefore visitors should spend some time learning about it before traveling there. Visitors can guarantee that their time in Luxembourg is enjoyable and courteous by adhering to the country's cultural customs.

As a visitor, I found Luxembourg's cultural etiquette to be quite helpful. I took the effort to study some common phrases in Luxembourgish and was extremely aware of the importance of speaking the right language when interacting with locals. I also took great care to honor religious traditions by dressing modestly and refraining from public demonstrations of affection. When chatting with locals, I also took care to be courteous and respectful, speaking at a reasonable volume and using the words "please" and "thank you" when appropriate. Overall, I found Luxembourg's citizens to be incredibly hospitable and friendly, and I had a lovely time there.

I would advise visitors to Luxembourg to spend some time getting acquainted with the customs and etiquette of the nation. This entails being kind and respectful while engaging with locals, learning at least a few simple phrases in Luxembourgish, and respecting religious practices. Furthermore, visitors should be patient and sympathetic because it may take Luxembourgers some time to warm up to newcomers. Visitors can guarantee that their time in Luxembourg is enjoyable and courteous by adhering to the country's cultural customs.

DINING ETIQUETTE

It's crucial to be aware of the local protocol while eating out in Luxembourg. Even while Luxembourg's eating traditions are relatively comparable to those of other regions of Europe, you should be aware of a few minor variations.

The first thing to keep in mind is to dress correctly while eating in Luxembourg. Arriving at a restaurant with casual attire, such as jeans and a t-shirt, is frowned upon. Instead, make an effort to dress more formally by donning a dress or a suit.

It is typical to order an appetizer and a main entrée when you get the menu. You may even choose a three-course dinner if you like since many places provide it. It is usually normal to order a bottle of wine with your dinner, but if you're unclear about what to choose, be sure to ask your waitress for advice.

It's vital to wait until everyone at the table has been served before diving in when your meal comes out. It's also considerate to hold off on starting your dinner until the host or hostess has finished theirs.

The host or hostess will normally take care of the bill when it comes to paying it. However, it is considerate to offer to pay if you are the guest. Although Luxembourg dining etiquette is not difficult, understanding and observing these rules can help you have a nice and happy meal experience.

Finally, it's crucial to remember to say goodbye to your host or hostess and thank your waiter before leaving.

Dining manners that a first-time visitor to Luxembourg should be aware of:

1. Don the proper attire. Arriving at a restaurant with casual attire, such as jeans and a t-shirt, is frowned upon. Instead, make an effort to dress more formally by donning a dress or a suit.

2. Place a starter and entrée order. You may even choose a three-course dinner if you like since many places provide it.

3. Add a bottle of wine to your dining order.

4. Don't start eating until everyone at the table has been served.

5. Usually, the host or hostess foots the cost.

6. When you depart, thank your host or hostess and bid them farewell.

TRAVEL REQUIREMENTS

As one of the most well-liked vacation spots in Europe, Luxembourg offers stunning beauty, a distinct culture, and a rich history. Before making travel plans, tourists should be informed of Luxembourg's travel restrictions.

As a signatory to the Schengen Agreement, Luxembourg does not need a visa for entry from nationals of other Schengen Area nations. You must, however, get a visa in advance of traveling if you are a citizen of a non-Schengen nation.

You must have a passport that is currently valid and has at least three months remaining on it after your intended departure date from Luxembourg if you are coming from outside the Schengen Area. A valid return ticket and documentation of enough finances are also required. You should also consider getting travel insurance.

Visitors are permitted to import a reasonable quantity of products for personal use without incurring customs fees. On other things, however, including plants and animals, weapons, explosives, and medicines, there are limitations.

Visitors to Luxembourg must also be familiar with the local rules and laws. The majority of nations demand that tourists have a current passport, but Luxembourg additionally demands that they register with their neighborhood police station within three days of arriving.

Finally, before visiting Luxembourg, travelers should be informed of the local currency and exchange rate. You may get exchange rates online or at the airport. The native currency is the Euro. It's also vital to remember that Luxembourg accepts credit cards extensively.

You may guarantee a secure and pleasurable journey to Luxembourg by adhering to these travel rules. Luxembourg has plenty to offer everyone, whether you want a relaxing getaway or an exciting experience. Start your travel arrangements now to enjoy everything that Luxembourg has to offer.

The travel requirements for Luxembourg were quite simple when I recently went there as a tourist. I found it quite handy because I did not need to get a visa to visit the country since I am a citizen of a Schengen Area nation.

I was permitted to import a decent quantity of items for my use by customs. I registered with the neighborhood police station three days after arriving since I was also aware of the rules and legislation in the area.

The local currency is the Euro, and credit cards are commonly accepted, so I found money conversion to be rather simple. Overall, I had a nice vacation and had a great experience with the travel requirements for Luxembourg.

I would encourage visitors visiting Luxembourg to make sure they have a passport that is current and has at least three months remaining on it after their intended date of departure from Luxembourg. It's also crucial to have a valid return ticket and confirmation of adequate finances. Additionally, I would advise travelers to get travel insurance.

Before traveling to Luxembourg, I would advise travelers to familiarize themselves with the country's laws and regulations, as well as any limitations on certain goods like plants, animals, firearms, explosives, and narcotics.

- Visitors must register with the local police station within three days of arrival and must have a valid passport that is valid for at least three months beyond their intended date of departure from Luxembourg.
- The local currency is the Euro, and credit cards are generally accepted.
- Visitors are permitted to bring in a decent number of products for personal use, however, there are prohibitions on other things such as plants, animals, weapons, explosives, and narcotics.
- It's against the law to smoke in public places and consume alcohol in public.
- Photographing military sites or certain government structures is prohibited.

• Buying, possessing, or using any kind of illicit substances is prohibited, as is operating a vehicle while under the influence of alcohol or narcotics.

• Driving a car without a current driver's license is prohibited.

Finally, although credit cards are commonly accepted in Luxembourg and the native currency is the Euro, I would still suggest travelers examine these topics before traveling there. Tourists may guarantee a secure and comfortable journey to Luxembourg by following these instructions.

TRAVEL RESTRICTIONS

The severe but comforting travel restrictions in Luxembourg were extremely onerous. I had to fill out a health questionnaire upon arrival and show a COVID-19 PCR test that had come back negative within the previous 72 hours. In addition, I had to sign an attestation confirming that I am aware of the hazards involved with travel and wear a face mask while in public. The Luxembourg government's contact tracking smartphone app helped me to simply keep track of my locations throughout my visit, so I was pleasantly delighted to learn that I could use it. Overall, because of the stringent travel restrictions in place, I felt quite protected and well taken care of throughout my time in Luxembourg.

1. All visitors to Luxembourg must provide proof of a COVID-19 PCR test result obtained no more than 72 hours before their arrival.

2. Every tourist must sign up and give contact details for Luxembourg's contact tracking app.

3. A health questionnaire for all visitors is required to be completed before departure.

4. Face masks must be worn in public by all passengers.

5. Attending big gatherings, including religious events, is forbidden for all tourists.

6. Upon arrival, each passenger is required to sign an attestation acknowledging the hazards of their journey.

7. A 10-day quarantine is imposed upon admission for all visitors from nations or areas where COVID-19 is very prevalent.

8. Each passenger is required to provide a current passport and evidence of adequate finances to cover their stay.

9. Entry temperature checks are required for all visitors.

10. Every traveler is required to download and utilize the contact tracking mobile app from the government of Luxembourg.

Luxembourg's travel limitations were rather nice. Every stage of the procedure, from the health questionnaire before arrival to the temperature checks upon entering, thoroughly explained the constraints. Knowing that the government was making the necessary preparations to provide a secure atmosphere for guests, I felt comfortable and protected. The contact tracing app was also very useful because it made it simple for me to monitor my whereabouts while I was there. Overall, I felt at ease with Luxembourg's travel limitations since they were well-planned.

I would urge fellow tourists to be aware that rigorous travel restrictions are in place in Luxembourg to ensure everyone's safety. Bring a COVID-19 PCR test result that was negative within the previous 72 hours, register with Luxembourg's contact tracing app, finish a health questionnaire, put on a face mask in public, and sign an attestation when you arrive. To track your whereabouts during your visit, be sure to download and use the Luxembourg government's contact tracing mobile app. These actions will guarantee a secure and comfortable trip to Luxembourg.

UNDERSTANDING FOREIGN CURRENCY AND TRANSACTIONS

Luxembourg is a stunning nation in Europe with a vibrant past and present. Tourists find it to be a desirable location, and the Euro is a big appeal. Many nations in the Eurozone utilize the euro, which is the official currency of Luxembourg.

The value of the euro is anticipated to stay high over the long run since it is a dependable and stable currency. Due to its widespread acceptance across Europe, the euro is a preferred form of payment for visitors and travelers. The most extensively used currency in Luxembourg is the euro, which is also the preferred currency for many companies.

In Luxembourg, using the euro is straightforward. The nation is devoted to its currency and is a member of the Eurozone. This indicates that all shops, eateries, and lodging facilities accept the euro. Any bank or bureau de change will convert local cash for euros for travelers. In addition to being practical and stable, the euro is also quite economical. Luxembourg has one of the lowest costs of livings in the Eurozone, and its pricing for products and services is reasonable. This implies that tourists may take advantage of Luxembourg while still having a good time.

Because it is simple to convert, the euro is a fantastic alternative for visitors visiting

Luxembourg. The euro is widely accepted across the Eurozone, making transfers and purchases from neighboring nations simple. This makes it the perfect option for those who wish to maximize their vacation budget.

In Luxembourg, the euro is a fantastic currency for visitors. It offers excellent value for the money and is dependable and steady. Additionally, it is simple to use and accepted in a large number of Eurozone nations. A euro is a great option for those who want to get the most out of their money while in Luxembourg.

There are several simple ways to calculate the currency if you're a first-time visitor to Luxembourg.

The first thing you should do is to become familiar with the euro and Luxembourgish franc exchange rates. Most banks and currency exchange kiosks offer this exchange rate. You can convert your currency into euros using an online calculator once you know the exchange rate.

Utilizing a credit card is an additional simple method of calculating the currency. When you make a purchase, the majority of credit cards will automatically convert your local currency into euros. This method of calculating the currency is practical and straightforward.

You can go to a bank or a kiosk that offers currency exchange if you prefer to do it in person. You may exchange your local cash for euros at these places. This is a great way to determine the exchange rate and calculate the currency.

Finally, if you're visiting Luxembourg, you can also withdraw money from an ATM there. This is a terrific approach to ensure that you obtain the best exchange rate and have cash on hand for emergencies.

Here are some tips if you're thinking about investing in Luxembourg.

First, be sure to conduct your homework and comprehend the Luxembourg investing environment. It's critical to comprehend the numerous investing options, prospective risks and benefits, and applicable laws. It's crucial to comprehend how investing in Luxembourg will affect your taxes.

It's crucial to build a diverse portfolio after doing your homework and learning about the Luxembourg investing environment. Diversification lowers risk while raising possible benefits. Think about stock, bond, and commodity investments, as well as nontraditional ones like venture capital and real estate.

It's also critical to monitor Luxembourg's political and economic environment. Keep yourself informed of any developments that could affect your finances.

Last but not least, be sure to deal with a knowledgeable financial counselor. Your objectives and level of risk tolerance may be taken into account when developing an investment plan with the assistance of a seasoned and trustworthy financial adviser.

A fantastic approach to diversify your portfolio and maybe earn returns is by investing in Luxembourg. But it's crucial to do your homework, build a diverse portfolio, and consult a seasoned financial counselor.

CONSIDERING USING SIM OR WIFI IN LUXEMBOURG

Luxembourg is a wonderful place to visit and discover as a visitor. Despite its modest size, Luxembourg has a lot to offer, like the Sim and WiFi of Luxembourg. Getting online is necessary whether you're traveling for leisure or business.

The good news is that Europe's greatest mobile and wifi alternatives are available in

Luxembourg. The nation is home to a top-notch mobile network and a variety of wifi hotspots. You may access the Internet whenever you want and take advantage of everything that the digital world has to offer with the help of Luxembourg's SIM and WiFi.

Luxembourg's Sim and WiFi provide dependable and quick connections. All major cities are covered by the mobile network, which is one of the greatest in all of Europe. Remote places and rural areas may also use Luxembourg's SIM and WiFi. This makes it simple to keep in touch even when you're in a distant area.

The Sim and WiFi of Luxembourg provide affordable prices and top-notch customer support. You may pick the ideal plan for your requirements from a variety of plans that vary from basic to more sophisticated packages. Additionally, the Sim and WiFi in Luxembourg provide excellent value. With no additional fees or hidden costs, you may access the Internet for a reasonable price.

Luxembourg's Sim and WiFi also provide a ton of other advantages. For instance, you may make inexpensive international calls using your Sim. A variety of internet services are also available to you, including email, social networking, and streaming.

Additionally safe and dependable are Luxembourg's Sim and WiFi. You may be confident that your data is safe and secure since the mobile network is very secure and protected.

To secure your data, the wifi hotspots also use cutting-edge encryption technologies.

Overall, travelers get good service from Luxembourg's SIM and WiFi. You can remain connected and take advantage of the digital world with quick, dependable connections at affordable prices. With Luxembourg's SIM and WiFi, you can fully enjoy your visit and take advantage of all the country has to offer.

I had a terrific experience with the SIM and WiFi as a visitor visiting Luxembourg for the first time. The mobile network was quick and dependable, and it had great coverage in all the main cities. I was able to access the Internet at a reasonable price thanks to the WiFi and Sim, which both offered excellent value for the money.

The additional features of the Sim and WiFi were also quite useful in my opinion. For instance, I had access to a variety of internet services, including social media and streaming, and I could make cheap international calls. A major comfort was that the wifi hotspots employed cutting-edge encryption technology to protect my data.

My overall impression of Luxembourg's SIM and WiFi was favorable. Without any problems or concerns, I was able to remain connected and take advantage of the digital world. I was able to fully enjoy my vacation and see everything that Luxembourg has to offer thanks to the SIM and WiFi of Luxembourg.

I would suggest anybody wishing to use their SIM card and WiFi in Luxembourg to conduct their homework and select the best deal for their need. From simple to more complex packages, Luxembourg provides a broad selection of options. It's critical to evaluate costs and choose the greatest deals.

I would also advise making use of the further advantages that Luxembourg's SIM and WiFi provided. For instance, you may access a variety of internet services, including streaming and social media, and make inexpensive international calls. To secure your data, the wifi hotspots also use cutting-edge encryption technologies.

Last but not least, I'd suggest double-checking the coverage in the places you're traveling to. All major towns and rural regions are covered by Luxembourg's WiFi and SIM, so keeping connected shouldn't be a problem. To be on the safe side, it's always a good idea to research the coverage in the region you're traveling.

The Places To Get The Sim And Its Cost

There are several locations where visitors visiting Luxembourg may get a Sim. The three most common locations to purchase a SIM card are online, at local cell phone stores, and airports.

You may purchase a prepaid plan and a Sim card at mobile phone stores. Many stores provide excellent customer service and affordable pricing.

You may purchase a Sim card at the airport from one of the various kiosks. Although they are often more costly than phone stores, they might be a practical choice for visitors to Luxembourg.

You can now purchase a Sim card online. Sim cards are available at affordable costs on several websites. Sim cards are also available from both local and foreign vendors, including Lycamobile and Orange.

Overall, there are several locations in Luxembourg where you may get a Sim as a visitor. It's critical to evaluate costs and choose the greatest deals.

Depending on the carrier and the plan you choose, a Sim card in Luxembourg may cost anywhere from EUR 10 to EUR 100. Although pricing might vary based on the plan and provider, most Sim cards start at roughly €5.

For instance, Lycamobile has a basic package with 2GB of data and unlimited calls for €5. Orange also provides a selection of bundles, starting at €9.99 for 2GB and going up to €19.99 for 6GB.

The price of a Sim card in Luxembourg is often rather reasonable. It's critical to evaluate costs and choose the greatest deals.

VACCINATION NEEDED

It's crucial to make sure your immunizations are current if you're a tourist visiting Luxembourg. A variety of dangerous ailments and diseases, even those that would be uncommon in your own country, can be prevented with vaccinations. Fortunately, Luxembourg provides a broad choice of free or inexpensive vaccinations for tourists, making it simple to be safe while traveling there.

You should refresh your immunizations against common diseases including tetanus, polio, and diphtheria before visiting Luxembourg. It's crucial to take into account the dangers of other diseases, such as Hepatitis A, which may be acquired by consuming tainted food or water.

Consider getting this disease's vaccine, especially if you'll be traveling to or staying in remote or unsanitary places.

Visitors visiting Luxembourg should think about getting the seasonal influenza vaccine in addition to immunizations for common diseases. This is especially crucial for visitors who come during the winter when influenza is most prevalent. The flu may be uncomfortable and sometimes even deadly, but the influenza vaccination can help keep you from getting it.

Finally, it's crucial to keep in mind that, although being a safe country to visit, Luxembourg may have certain places where the danger of contracting certain diseases is greater. It's crucial to check that your vaccines are current and to do some study on the area's health dangers before traveling there.

Immunizations are generally a crucial component of being healthy and secure when traveling in Luxembourg. Before your trip, make sure your immunizations are current and learn about any potential health hazards in the region you'll be visiting. By doing this, you may relax on your vacation to Luxembourg and not worry about becoming sick.

Since I was a little kid, I have followed my doctor's advice and had the prescribed regular immunizations. I had the MMR, chickenpox, and influenza vaccinations as a child to protect me from a variety of diseases. As an adult, I make it a point to stay current on my immunizations and receive the seasonal flu shot every year. I recently visited a poor nation as well, so I made sure to receive the proper immunizations to guard myself against diseases like Hepatitis A. I am thankful that I have access to vaccinations since they have played a crucial role in my life.

I would encourage folks to confirm that their immunizations are current. Before traveling to a foreign country or indulging in any activities that might raise your risk of catching a disease, it is crucial to make sure that your vaccines are up to date. Vaccines can protect you against a variety of deadly illnesses. Additionally, it's crucial to check that your vaccines are current and learn about any potential health hazards in the region you'll be traveling. Finally, I would advise discussing any further immunizations that could be required for your specific circumstances with your doctor.

CHAPTER TWO

GETTING TO LUXEMBOURG

Despite being a tiny European nation, Luxembourg is one of the most popular travel destinations. It's hardly surprising that this little nation attracts millions of travelers each year given its breathtaking scenery, historical sites, and lively culture.

You're in for a big treat if you want to organize a vacation to Luxembourg. There are many sites to visit, from the stunning medieval towns of the Moselle Valley to the magnificent castles of the Ardennes.

As it is linked to many significant European cities, getting to Luxembourg is not too difficult. There are several direct flights from the UK, Germany, France, and other nearby nations to Luxembourg Airport, where you may travel. As an alternative, you may travel across Luxembourg by bus and rail, including to the capital, Luxembourg City.

You will be astounded by the sheer volume of things to do, see, and experience once you arrive in Luxembourg. There is something for everyone, whether you want to stroll around Vianden's historic center or take a sail along the Moselle River. The Grand Ducal Palace, the Old City of Luxembourg, and the Luxembourg Citadel are just a few of the historical sites that can be found in Luxembourg.

There are many things to participate in if you want a special experience. Outdoor pursuits available in Luxembourg include skiing, motorcycling, hiking, and rock climbing. You may also attend a variety of cultural events or visit the many museums and galleries spread out over the city.

Whatever brought you to Luxembourg, you will undoubtedly have a memorable time. It's hardly surprising that this little nation attracts millions of tourists each year given its breathtaking scenery, historical sites, and lively culture.

Recently, I had a tourist trip to Luxembourg, and it was an amazing experience. I took a direct flight from London to Luxembourg Airport, and the trip went without a hitch. I was astounded by the breathtaking scenery and important historical sites when I arrived.

The Grand Ducal Palace, the Ancient City of Luxembourg, and the Citadel of Luxembourg were among the attractions I saw while spending a lot of time in the old city of Luxembourg. I also engaged in outdoor pursuits including riding, hiking, and rock climbing.

I got the chance to visit several cultural events and was particularly pleased with Luxembourg's lively culture. To understand more about the history and culture of the nation, I also went to a few of the nearby museums and art galleries.

Overall, Luxembourg was a great place to visit, and I heartily agree with your recommendation.

If you're visiting Luxembourg for the first time, I suggest taking some time to explore the beautiful landscapes and important historical sites of the nation. Visit some of the historic areas, including Vianden, the Grand Ducal Palace, and the Luxembourg Citadel.

Additionally, I advise participating in outdoor pursuits like bicycling, hiking, and rock climbing. It's also worthwhile to spend some time participating in some of the cultural activities, going to the nearby galleries and museums, and eating some of the regional food.

Finally, be sure to take some time to unwind and enjoy Luxembourg's beauty. You'll undoubtedly have a wonderful time, whether you want to take a boat along the Moselle River or just relax with a cup of coffee in one of the numerous nearby cafés.

friendly budget tips

I would advise making travel arrangements in advance if you want to visit Luxembourg on a tight budget. This will enable you to compare costs and discover the best offers for travel, lodging, and activities.

Additionally, try to purchase your train tickets in advance as they are frequently much less expensive than those purchased at the station. Look for discounts for students as well as special offers on regional attractions like museums and galleries.

Purchasing a Luxembourg Card, which grants you free access to public transportation and discounts to attractions, is worthwhile if you're visiting Luxembourg for a few days. Additionally, you can benefit from the numerous free events and activities that are offered all year long.

Last but not least, don't forget to indulge in all of Luxembourg's delectable culinary offerings. You can either purchase fresh ingredients from the nearby markets or visit one of the many restaurants to sample the regional fare.

CONSIDERABLE MEANS OF GETTING TO LUXEMBOURG AND THEIR PRICES:

1. Bus: If you're a tourist, buses are a terrific method to go to Luxembourg. Numerous businesses, including regional operators and multinational corporations, provide regular services from different regions of Europe. Prices for buses to Luxembourg may vary from €20 to €50 depending on the provider and route.

2. Train: Tourists often use trains to go to Luxembourg. Regular direct trains run from major cities including Paris, Brussels, London, Amsterdam, and more to Luxembourg from the majority of European nations. Depending on the operator and route, train tickets to Luxembourg may cost anywhere from €30 to €100.

3. Car: Those who possess their cars or are prepared to hire one may go to Luxembourg by driving there. The travel is enjoyable and hassle-free since the roads are well-maintained and well-marked.

4. Aircraft: Flying is the most expedient means of transportation to Luxembourg. With frequent flights to major European cities including London, Paris, and Amsterdam, Luxembourg is home to several significant airports. Ticket costs to Luxembourg vary based on the airline, route, and season, but often run between €50 and €200.

I recently traveled to Luxembourg as a tourist and discovered that the trip was rather simple and affordable. I decided to go by bus from my own country since the tickets ranged in price from €20 to €50. I quickly reached Luxembourg after a nice and enjoyable trip. To anybody searching for a convenient method to travel on a tight budget to Luxembourg, I would suggest this means of transportation.

WHEN TO VISIT LUXEMBOURG

Luxembourg should be at the top of your list when choosing a location for your next vacation. Tourists may enjoy the breathtaking natural beauty, vibrant culture, and fascinating history of this little European country. Luxembourg is a great holiday spot for anybody seeking an action-packed and memorable getaway since there is so much to see and do there.

The summer (June to August), when the weather is nice and the days are long, is the ideal season to visit Luxembourg. The country's outdoor attractions, like its numerous parks and hiking trails, are ideal to enjoy at this time of year. Due to the temperate temperatures and active ski season, the winter months may also be an excellent time to go to Luxembourg.

There will always be activities to keep you busy if you decide to visit Luxembourg at any time. The Grand Ducal Palace, Neumunster Abbey, and the National Museum of History are just a few of the intriguing sites in Luxembourg City, the country's capital. Discover the ancient town's maze of twisting cobblestone lanes and impressive buildings. A day excursion to the adjacent Moselle Valley is another option, where you may see charming vineyards and sip some of the area's well-known wines.

There are several top-notch museums and galleries in Luxembourg. Art aficionados must visit both the Museum of Modern Art and the National Museum of Art and History. To discover more about the region's varied fauna and ecosystem, visit the National Museum of Natural History.

You'll have a great time in Luxembourg whenever you decide to go there. Anyone wishing for a memorable and fulfilling vacation will find Luxembourg to be the perfect location, thanks to both its beautiful scenery and its dynamic culture.

My time in Luxembourg as a tourist was simply amazing. I spent a week there and was astounded by how charming it was. My days were spent wandering the narrow cobblestone alleys of Luxembourg City, admiring the Grand Ducal Palace's beautiful architecture, and taking in the breathtaking vistas of the Moselle Valley.

I also got to participate in a few cultural activities, such as the Grand Duchy of Luxembourg's National Day celebration. I also got to try some of the famous wines from the area and some authentic Luxembourgish food.

Overall, my trip to Luxembourg as a tourist was one of the best trips I have ever made. I heartily suggest it to everyone searching for a special and unforgettable vacation since it is an incredibly beautiful nation that is rich in history and culture.

Nice Places To Explore In Summer Months:

1. Grand Ducal Palace - The Grand Ducal Palace is an impressive structure with grand architecture and a lovely garden that is situated in the center of Luxembourg City.

2. Neumunster Abbey, one of the most significant ecclesiastical monuments in the nation, is a wonderful example of Gothic and Renaissance architecture.

3. National Museum of History - This museum, which has objects from antiquity to the present, lets you explore Luxembourg's rich history and culture.

4. The Old Town - Wander through the Old Town's winding alleyways made of cobblestones, which are lined with beautiful restaurants and cafés.

5. Vianden Castle - With its magnificent medieval architecture, lovely grounds, and breathtaking vistas, this castle is a must-see for every traveler.

6. Echternach - Explore this little town's historic abbey, one of the oldest in all of Europe.

7. Moselle Valley - Spend the day exploring the breathtaking Moselle Valley, where you can take in the gorgeous vineyards and try some of the area's world-famous wines.

8. The National Museum of Art and History is home to a vast collection of artwork and artifacts from all around the globe.

9. Museum of Modern Art - Discover contemporary art at this gallery, which showcases pieces by some of the most well-known modern painters in the world.

10. Parc Merveilleux - Wander around this lovely park and take in the gardens, rides, and other features.

Finally, Luxembourg has a lot to offer outdoor enthusiasts. There's something for everyone, from hiking and biking in the Ardennes to kayaking down the Moselle River. For those looking to get away from it all, the country's numerous lakes and parks are ideal places to unwind and take in the breathtaking scenery.

Luxembourg is the place to go if you want to have a memorable vacation. You're sure to have an unforgettable experience with its mix of culture, outdoor activities, and stunning scenery. So why not start planning your vacation to Luxembourg right now?

WHERE TO STAY IN LUXEMBOURG

A little nation in central Europe called Luxembourg provides a remarkable fusion of culture and natural beauty. Luxembourg has something for everyone, whether you want to tour its magnificent castles, taste some of the greatest food in Europe, or just unwind and take in the amazing vistas. Therefore, the best lodgings that you should take into consideration if you're looking for the ideal place to stay in Luxembourg are listed below.

In Luxembourg City, the Grand Hotel Cravat is the ideal option for visitors looking for an opulent experience. The hotel's rooftop terrace and suites provide breathtaking city views and are located right in the center of the city. You'll experience five-star service, cutting-edge conveniences, and luxurious decor during your stay.

The Adolphe Bridge Hotel is a great option if you want something more reasonably priced. This hotel, which is situated in Luxembourg, has a welcoming atmosphere, helpful staff, and a good location. You can easily explore the city because many of the city's top attractions are close to the hotel.

The Chateau de Vianden is the ideal choice if you're looking for a distinctive place to stay. This castle provides a one-of-a-kind experience and is situated in the stunning Vianden valley. This is a truly unique place to stay with its opulent suites, medieval accents, and breathtaking views of the surrounding countryside.

Finally, the Villa des Roses is the ideal accommodation for those seeking a more private stay. This charming hotel has stunning views of the Moselle River and is situated in a rural area close to Greven Macher. Villa des Roses is the ideal place to unwind with its cozy lodgings and serene ambiance.

Luxembourg offers a variety of accommodations, no matter what kind you're looking for. There are many wonderful places to stay in Luxembourg, whether you're looking for an opulent stay or a more affordable option. So begin making travel arrangements for this lovely nation, and find the ideal lodging.

LUXURY ACCOMMODATION

Luxurious high-end accommodations are available in Luxembourg, a stunning nation in the center of Europe, and they provide the ideal balance of flair and comfort. There is something for everyone in Luxembourg, from the recognizable Grand Ducal Palace to the lovely Belvedere Palace.

The Grand Ducal Palace is the ideal spot to stay for people seeking the height of luxury. The palace, which is in the center of the city, provides astonishingly magnificent apartments with fine furniture and opulent extras. The Grand Ducal Museum, located inside the palace, offers tourists a look into the past of Luxembourg and its royal family.

The Belvedere Palace is the best choice for a more modern stay. The palace, which is situated in the picturesque district of Grund, provides contemporary, fashionable rooms as well as a variety of upscale facilities. Take a walk around the lovely grounds or get a treatment at the spa and health center. The palace also has a substantial collection of artwork, including pieces by both national and foreign artists.

And last, for those seeking more opulent accommodation, the Four Seasons Hotel Luxembourg is a fantastic option. The hotel, which is in the heart of the city, has luxurious facilities, cutting-edge accommodations, and a fine dining establishment. The hotel's rooftop patio, which provides breathtaking views of the city, is also available to guests.

1. Grand Hotel Cravat – Located in Luxembourg City

In the center of Luxembourg City stands the opulent four-star Grand Hotel Cravat. The hotel has a beautiful perspective of the city and is ideally close to popular sights, eateries, and shops.

A spa and wellness center, a swimming pool, and a fitness facility are just a few of the contemporary facilities available at Grand Hotel Cravat. The hotel also has a restaurant, a lounge, and a bar, among other eating choices.

The hotel offers a variety of lodging options, including suites and regular rooms. Modern décor and cozy furniture are found in every room. Satellite TV and Wi-Fi are also offered without charge to visitors.

The 24-hour front desk, laundry service, and concierge are just a few of the amenities provided by Grand Hotel Cravat. A shuttle service from the hotel to the airport and other areas of the city is also available.

Grand Hotel Cravat is a great option for those looking for an opulent place to stay in Luxembourg City. The hotel offers visitors a luxurious experience with its first-rate facilities and services.

The Grand Hotel Cravat's nightly rate varies according to the kind and size of the room, as well as the time of year. Standard rooms start at €79 per night, while suites start at €399 per night.

2. Chateau De Vianden – Located In The Valley Of Vianden

One of Luxembourg's most magnificent and stunning castles is Chateau De Vianden. The castle, which is situated in the lovely Vianden valley, was built in the 10th century and has played a significant role in Luxembourg's history ever since. For many years, this magnificent castle has served as the center of authority and power, and it has seen several kings come and go.

The top, middle, and lower castles make form the whole structure. The primary living quarters were situated in the upper castle, which is the oldest. Over the years, the middle and lower castles were erected, serving as fortifications and bolstering the castle's defensive strength.

The castle, which sits on a steep hill and looks out over the town of Vianden, is encircled by high walls and a moat. You can see for kilometers in every direction from the castle's walls and turrets. Over the years, the castle underwent renovations and restorations and is now accessible to the public.

A museum with numerous historical objects may be found within the castle walls. You may also go about the castle grounds, which include secluded paths and lovely gardens.

A must-see for anybody traveling to Luxembourg is the Chateau De Vianden, a magnificent illustration of the splendor of medieval architecture. It is a great location to visit and discover the area's history.

Depending on the kind of lodging you choose, a night at Chateau De Vianden will cost a certain amount. Rooms, apartments, and villas are some of the rental choices offered. The cost each night ranges from €50 to €200. There might also be extra charges like cleaning fees and tourist taxes.

3. Hotel Le Place d'Armes – Located in Luxembourg City

The luxurious and magnificent Hotel Le Place d'Armes is situated in the center of Luxembourg City. The hotel provides a great starting point for visiting the city and its surroundings since it is located in the stunning Grand Duchy of Luxembourg.

A variety of lodging choices, including standard and superior rooms, junior suites, and luxury suites, are available at the hotel, which is housed in a 19th-century structure. Modern conveniences including free Wi-Fi, flat-screen TVs, air conditioning, and private bathrooms are provided for guests.

In addition, the hotel offers a variety of recreational amenities, such as a sauna, a fitness center, and a restaurant offering a variety of different cuisines. A bar and a personal garden are also present.

The Notre Dame Cathedral, the Grand Ducal Palace, and the museums are a few of the city's top attractions that are near Hotel Le Place d'Armes since it is situated in the city's center. Additionally, visitors may participate in a variety of activities, such as cycling and hiking.

The ideal location for a luxurious getaway in Luxembourg City, Hotel Le Place d'Armes provides excellent value for money.

The average nightly rate for a regular room at Hotel Le Place d'Armes in Luxembourg City is €86.

4. Parc Hotel – Located in the city of Luxembourg

The Parc Hotel is situated in the tiny European nation of Luxembourg, which is sandwiched between France, Germany, and Belgium. A luxury 4-star hotel, it provides upscale amenities, first-rate guest support, and a prime position in the heart of the city.

All of the contemporary conveniences and facilities are provided in the hotel's rooms. A unique stay is guaranteed by the private balconies found in every room, which provide beautiful views of the downtown skyline. Visitors may stroll to a range of sites and activities including museums, shops, and entertainment venues from the hotel.

Delicious local and foreign food is served in the hotel's restaurant, and a good range of wines and spirits are kept on hand in the bar. The hotel's spa and wellness center also offer guests the chance to indulge in a soothing massage or spa service.

For travel or work, the Parc Hotel is fantastic accommodation. It is well suited for individuals who wish to discover everything that Luxembourg has to offer because of its accessible location in the center of the city.

Depending on the kind of accommodation you reserve and the season, the price per night at the Parc Hotel varies. The price per night for a typical single room is between €150 and €200. The price each night for a double or a family room is between €200 and €250.

5. Sofitel Luxembourg Le Grand Ducal – Located in Luxembourg City

Luxurious lodgings may be found at the Sofitel Luxembourg Le Grand Ducal in the center of Luxembourg City. With its opulent services and facilities, this hotel offers a distinctive experience. It has a distinctive ambiance that is both chic and cozy thanks to its exquisite design and contemporary furnishings.

To suit every budget, the hotel provides a selection of rooms and suites. With several conveniences to make your stay pleasant, the rooms are roomy and airy. Every room has a balcony with a lovely view of the city. A wide range of services is also provided by the hotel to enhance your enjoyment of your stay. These consist of a restaurant, spa, swimming pool, and fitness facility.

The hotel provides visitors with a variety of activities in addition to first-rate lodging and services. There is something for everyone, from shopping and eating to biking and kayaking.

The Sofitel Luxembourg Le Grand Ducal is the ideal option if you want a luxurious hotel stay in

Luxembourg City. This hotel will undoubtedly enhance the quality of your visit to Luxembourg City with its outstanding facilities and services.

The Sofitel Luxembourg Le Grand Ducal offers rooms starting at €175 per night.

6. Chateau de Bourglinster – Located in the countryside near the Moselle River

Beautiful Château de Bourglinster is situated in Luxembourg's rural area close to the Moselle River. This wonderful, old house was built in the thirteenth century and has stunning views of the countryside. While exploring the lovely grounds and gardens, visitors can savor the peaceful ambiance, delectable cuisine, and opulent accommodations.

People who want to experience the allure of a traditional European castle frequently travel to the château. It has several bedrooms, each of which is well-furnished and equipped with contemporary facilities. The on-site restaurant, which offers a variety of regional dishes, as well as the bar are available to visitors.

The lovely gardens, the park, or the nearby village are all great options for those looking for things to do. Throughout the year, the château also hosts a variety of special events, such as wine tastings and musical performances.

Depending on the type of lodging selected, a stay at Château de Bourglinster starts at €140 per night. Additionally, guests may benefit from reduced costs for prolonged stays. Château de Bourglinster is the ideal getaway because of its stunning setting and opulent atmosphere.

7. Villa des Roses – Located in the countryside near Grevenmacher

The luxurious hotel Villa des Roses is situated in rural Luxembourg next to Grevenmacher. Visitors may find peace here as they escape the bustle of the city. From their balconies, guests may take in the breathtaking views of the undulating hills, lush woods, and sparkling rivers.

The hotel has 40 rooms, each of which is uniquely designed and furnished with contemporary conveniences. There is a comfortable lounge space, a flat-screen TV, and a mini-bar in every room. A restaurant, a bar, and a pool are on-site facilities.

Visitors may stay in comfort at Villa des Roses at a reasonable cost. A sumptuous continental breakfast is included in the nightly starting rate of only €80. Golf, hiking, and cycling are just a few of the activities that visitors may partake in. The hotel also provides a variety of spa treatments, including facials and massages.

For those seeking to go away to a tranquil rural setting, Villa des Roses is the ideal location. It's the perfect location to unwind and rejuvenate with its opulent facilities and breathtaking vistas.

8. Park Inn by Radisson Luxembourg City – Located in Luxembourg City

The Park Inn by Radisson Luxembourg City is a great place for those who want to see the city and its surrounds since it is centrally located. An indoor pool, fitness center, spa, and conference space are just a few of the hotel's opulent features. It also has a restaurant, a bar, and a business center for those who are on business trips.

The hotel provides cozy lodgings, including suites in addition to ordinary and superior rooms. Modern conveniences including flat-screen TVs, free Wi-Fi, and air conditioning are available in every room. Additionally, guests get free access to the spa and a complimentary breakfast each morning.

A normal room at the Park Inn by Radisson Luxembourg City costs €99 per night, while a suite costs €349 per night. For those searching for a longer stay, the hotel is a wonderful choice since it provides discounted prices for longer stays.

The Park Inn by Radisson Luxembourg City is a great choice whether you're searching for an opulent place to stay in the center of Luxembourg City or an accessible location from which to explore the area. You can expect a pleasant stay thanks to the hotel's contemporary facilities and ideal location.

9. Hotel Le Royal Luxembourg – Located in Luxembourg City

The Park Inn by Radisson Luxembourg City is a great place for those who want to see the city and its surrounds since it is centrally located. An indoor pool, fitness center, spa, and conference space are just a few of the hotel's opulent features. It also has a restaurant, a bar, and a business center for those who are on business trips.

The hotel provides cozy lodgings, including suites in addition to ordinary and superior rooms. Modern conveniences including flat-screen TVs, free Wi-Fi, and air conditioning are available in every room. Additionally, guests get free access to the spa and a complimentary breakfast each morning. A normal room at the Park Inn by Radisson Luxembourg City costs €99 per night, while a suite costs €349 per night. For those searching for a longer stay, the hotel is a wonderful choice since it provides discounted prices for longer stays. The Park Inn by Radisson Luxembourg City is a great choice whether you're searching for an opulent place to stay in the center of Luxembourg City or an accessible location from which to explore the area. You can expect an enjoyable stay thanks to the hotel's contemporary facilities and ideal location.

10. Hotel Le Chatelet – Located in Luxembourg City

In the center of Luxembourg City, the opulent 4-star Hotel Le Châtelet can be found. The hotel is ideal for those who want to discover the famous attractions of the city since it is close to the Grand Ducal Palace and the charming Adolphe Bridge.

The hotel offers contemporary, well-decorated rooms, each with air conditioning, a flat-screen TV, and a private bathroom. A restaurant, a bar, and a fitness facility are just a few of the extras available to visitors. To complete your stay, you may order room service.

Additional services provided by the hotel include laundry, dry cleaning, and a concierge service. The kind, accommodating staff of Hotel Le Châtelet is always on hand to see to your requirements.

The Grand Ducal Palace and Notre Dame Cathedral are only a short stroll from the hotel, as are other popular downtown sights. There are many different places to buy, eat, and have fun in Luxembourg City.

Depending on the style of accommodation and the duration of stay, a stay at Hotel Le Châtelet might cost anywhere from €125 and €200 per night. This makes it the perfect option for anybody seeking a comfortable and opulent place to stay in Luxembourg City.

FRIENDLY BUDGET

Luxurious hotels as well as more moderately priced and budget-friendly lodging alternatives may be found in Luxembourg. There are several possibilities for travelers on a tight budget who want to visit Luxembourg.

Hostels are among the most well-liked forms of inexpensive lodging in Luxembourg. Hostels provide cozy, affordable housing with public spaces and shared amenities. Basic services including Wi-Fi, a kitchen, a lounge space, and a gathering place are available in many hostels in Luxembourg. For single travelers, couples, and groups of friends searching for a comfortable and economical place to stay, hostels are perfect.

Apartments are a fantastic choice for low-cost lodging in Luxembourg. Many moderately priced rental flats in Luxembourg come with standard features like Wi-Fi and a kitchen. Families, couples, and groups of friends searching for a more private and intimate lodging option can choose apartments.

For individuals searching for inexpensive lodging in Luxembourg, hotels and guesthouses are excellent choices. Wi-Fi, a restaurant, and a bar are among the standard services that many hotels and guesthouses provide. They are perfect for families, friends, and couples searching for a cozy and economical place to stay.

1. Hostelling International Luxembourg

Travelers seeking a cozy, inexpensive, and secure place to stay in Luxembourg should consider Hostelling International Luxembourg. HI, Luxembourg is a centrally located hotel that provides a range of services and amenities to enhance your stay. Every room in the hostel has a private bathroom and free Wi-Fi, ranging from private rooms to shared dormitories. The communal kitchen, lounge, and bar are also available for guests to use at HI Luxembourg. The lounge has lots of comfortable seating, a TV, and books in addition the kitchen is fully equipped with everything you could need to prepare meals. There are several types of beers and spirits in the bar area, along with snacks and soft drinks. Additionally, HI Luxembourg offers a wide range of excursions and activities, including bike and boat rentals, guided city tours, and several cultural events. The nightly rates at HI Luxembourg are very affordable, with shared dormitory rooms starting at €15 and private rooms at €30. It's always worthwhile to check the HI Luxembourg website to see their current deals because prices vary depending on the season and availability.

2. Grand Hotel Cravat

In the center of Luxembourg City stands the opulent 4-star Grand Hotel Cravat. The hotel has a sleek, modern structure with a pleasant environment. Aside from a restaurant and bar, it also has a fitness facility, spa, and business center for the use of its visitors. The hotel also has a range of rooms and suites, all of which have contemporary furnishings and conveniences.

The rooms and suites of the Grand Hotel Cravat are reasonably priced. Prices for a basic double room start at €99 per night and go up to €400 for a suite. Modern conveniences like air conditioning, flat-screen TVs, and complimentary Wi-Fi are included in every accommodation. The hotel also provides several packages, including one that includes breakfast and supper or special prices for business guests.

If you want an opulent and pleasant place to stay in Luxembourg City, choose the Grand Hotel Cravat. A hotel is an excellent option for both business and leisure tourists since it provides a variety of services and reasonable rates.

3. Auberge de Jeunesse Luxembourg

The Auberge de Jeunesse Luxembourg is a fantastic alternative for tourists on a tight budget who want to see the lovely nation of Luxembourg. The hostel, which is in the center of the city, has several services including free WiFi, a kitchenette, and a common area. The majority of the city's sights and eateries are also accessible on foot.

The hostel offers a range of lodging choices, including private rooms and dormitories, to accommodate any budget. Dorm rooms cost between 25 and 30 euros per person per night, while private rooms cost between 40 and 50 euros per person per night. Longer stays are also eligible for discounts at the hostel.

Anyone looking to visit Luxembourg City on a budget can consider staying at the Auberge de Jeunesse Luxembourg. It is the ideal choice for budget tourists because of its handy location and reasonable rates.

4. Hotel Parc Plaza

In the center of Paris stands the opulent 4-star Hotel Parc Plaza. Travelers may easily experience all the sights and sounds of the City of Light from this handy position in the city center.

A gorgeous patio, a fitness center, a spa, and an onsite restaurant are just a few of the hotel's many features. The range of accommodation types available to guests includes anything from single and double rooms to suites and family rooms.

The Hotel Parc Plaza is renowned for its outstanding hospitality and service. The staff cares about the comfort and enjoyment of every visitor. Along with many other services and facilities, the hotel provides a 24-hour front desk, free Wi-Fi, and car rentals.

Depending on the facilities and room type, a night at Hotel Parc Plaza may cost anywhere from €120 and €390. Additionally, guests may benefit from the hotel's promotions and special deals, such as the "Stay 3 Nights and Pay 2" deal.

Hotel Parc Plaza is the ideal option for anyone seeking an opulent stay in the center of Paris. This hotel guarantees a memorable stay because of its amazing location, first-rate service, and affordable rates.

5. ibis Luxembourg Sud

In Luxembourg City, there is a hotel called Ibis Luxembourg Sud. It provides cozy, contemporary lodging with a range of facilities, including a restaurant, bar, and fitness center. The city's major attractions are accessible by foot from the hotel, which is located in the heart of the city.

Ibis Luxembourg Sud provides luxurious accommodations at affordable rates. Standard rooms, family rooms, and suites are just a few of the several types of accommodations that are available to guests. Flat-screen TVs, free Wi-Fi, and air conditioning are provided in every room.

International and regional food is served at the hotel's restaurant and bar. Breakfast, lunch, and supper menus are available at the restaurant, and the bar is open until late.

The hotel also offers a variety of business and leisure amenities, such as a gym, conference spaces, and a business center. Additionally, the hotel offers complimentary parking and a 24-hour reception.

Regular accommodation at Ibis Luxembourg Sud costs around €80 per night. Family rooms and suites cost a little more, but they provide outstanding value.

6. Domaine des Meuniers

In the southern French hills, Domaine des Meuniers is a lovely and isolated refuge. This lovely house, located in the heart of the Languedoc-Roussillon region, provides visitors with a pleasant and serene location for the ideal retreat.

The estate's beautiful grounds, which include a sizable garden and a swimming pool, are home to several cottages and villas that serve as the property's lodging. Each cottage offers a pleasant stay and has been meticulously refurbished in a typical French style. With contemporary facilities and stunning views of the surrounding countryside, the villas provide even more luxury.

The estate provides a range of entertainment options for visitors, including horseback riding, hiking, fishing, and cycling. A well-stocked bar is available for those who want to unwind with a few drinks, and the on-site restaurant offers a variety of regional foods and beverages.

The costs per night at Domaine des Meuniers are reasonable in light of the ideal location for relaxation and rejuvenation. A typical cottage runs around €80 per night, although a villa may cost up to €200. The estate's suites are offered for €400 per night for an opulent stay.

7. Hotel Parc Belle-Vue

Luxurious boutique hotel Hotel Parc Belle-Vue is located in the center of Brussels, Belgium. The hotel, which is in the heart of the action, is a fantastic choice for tourists seeking a posh and relaxing stay. The Hotel Parc Belle-Vue provides a memorable experience with its gorgeous building, traditional French décor, dedicated personnel, and contemporary conveniences.

The hotel offers a variety of services, including a sauna, a fitness center, and a restaurant. Each of the rooms has a flat-screen TV, free Wi-Fi, and comfy mattresses with private bathrooms. Additionally available to guests are the hotel's laundry facilities, concierge services, and 24-hour room service.

The cost of a stay at Hotel Parc Belle-Vue varies based on the season and the kind of accommodation. While premium suites may cost up to €400 per night, standard accommodations start at around €120.

Whether you're planning a business vacation or a romantic holiday, Hotel Parc Belle-Vue will satisfy your requirements. It's the ideal spot to stay in Brussels because of its superb location and opulent facilities.

8. Hotel de la Gare

In the center of Paris, there is a lovely hotel called Hotel de la Gare. It provides excellent value for the money and is ideal for anyone seeking a cozy, inexpensive place to stay in the city. The hotel's handy location near the Gare du Nord railway station makes it simple to reach the city's main attractions.

The hotel has a range of accommodation types available, from Standard doubles to Deluxe suites. Flat-screen TVs, free Wi-Fi, and en suite bathrooms are included in every accommodation. Other features and services offered by the hotel include a 24-hour front desk, a restaurant and bar, a business center, and a laundry service.

A Standard double room at Hotel de la Gare costs €60 per night, while a Deluxe suite costs €180. But before booking a reservation, make sure to check out the hotel's website since they often have deals and bundles available.

Overall, Hotel de la Gare is a great option for those looking for a cozy, cheap hotel in Paris. Hotel de la Gare is a fantastic option to enjoy the city of love on a budget thanks to its handy location and excellent service.

9. Hotel des Ardennes

The charming Ardennes area of France is home to the warm and welcoming hotel known as Hotel des Ardennes. The hotel provides breathtaking views of Charleville-Mézières, a neighboring city, as well as the Ardennes' undulating hills, woods, and valleys. Hotel des Ardennes is the perfect place for a weekend escape or a longer stay because of its contemporary facilities and handy location.

The hotel has a range of accommodation options to fit any price range. There are single, double, twin, and family rooms available for guests. Private bathrooms and contemporary conveniences like flat-screen TVs, air conditioning, and Wi-Fi are included in every room. In addition, the hotel has a range of eating alternatives, including a full-service restaurant and informal lounges.

The hotel is near several local attractions, including the Valley of the Meuse and the Ardennes Forest, and is just a short drive from the city of Charleville-Mézières. The area is well-known for its beautiful scenery and is a well-liked location for outdoor pursuits including horseback riding, bicycling, and hiking.

The kind of accommodation and duration of stay are two factors that affect the cost of a stay at Hotel des Ardennes. Single rooms typically cost roughly €60 per night, double rooms start at €90, twin rooms start at €100, and family rooms start at €120. Depending on the season, these costs might fluctuate.

Hotel des Ardennes is the ideal spot to stay whether you're planning an outdoor adventure or a romantic weekend away. For guests of all ages, this hotel will undoubtedly provide a delightful experience thanks to its contemporary facilities and exceptional location.

10. City Hotel

In the center of the city, there is a chic and opulent hotel choice called City Hotel. All of its visitors are given pleasant accommodations by City Hotel, which offers a variety of room kinds and services. The hotel provides a range of accommodation options, including single rooms and suites, all of which come with upscale features like free Wi-Fi, flat-screen TVs, and other contemporary conveniences. Additional amenities offered by City Hotel include a 24-hour front desk, a restaurant, and a bar.

The cost of a stay at City Hotel varies according to the season and the kind of room. Prices for single rooms start at roughly $100 per night, while suites may go as much as $250 per night. The time of year has an impact on prices as well, with summer months often being more expensive than winter months.

For those looking for an affordable place to stay in the city center, City Hotel is the ideal option. The City Hotel is among the top-value hotels in the area because of its cutting-edge features, excellent service, and affordable rates.

11. Hotel Schanzer

Munich, Germany is home to the opulent 4-star Hotel Schanzer. It gives simple access to public transit and is situated close to the city core. The hotel has a restaurant, an indoor pool, a spa, and a fitness center in addition to its 148-roomy, contemporary accommodations. Each room has free Wi-Fi, a minibar, a flat-screen TV, and air conditioning.

Business travelers will enjoy the hotel's many business services, which include conference spaces, a business center, and free parking. With top-notch service and affordable rates, the Hotel Schanzer provides visitors with a welcoming and unwinding environment. A normal double room costs €99 per night, a superior double costs €129, and a deluxe suite costs €159. Guests who make online reservations or stay for a longer period may also take advantage of special deals and packages.

The Hotel Schanzer is a great spot to stay in Munich overall. It is the ideal option for guests seeking a pleasant and comfortable stay in the city because of its cozy accommodations, first-rate facilities, and affordable rates.

12. Hotel Charmey

In the Swiss Alps in the Val de Charmey, there is a four-star hotel called Hotel Charmey. It offers visitors a unique experience of luxury and tranquility together with the breathtaking beauty of nature. The hotel provides visitors with the ideal location for a winter holiday since it is near the ski slopes.

The hotel provides a selection of contemporary, cozy rooms with views of the surroundings. Every room has a flat-screen TV and air conditioning, and many have balconies with views of the mountains. A restaurant, bar, spa, and fitness center are all available at the hotel.

The season and kind of accommodation affect the Hotel Charmey's nightly rates. Suites may cost more than CHF 500 per night, while basic accommodations start at around CHF 200.

In general, Hotel Charmey is an opulent location for anyone seeking a distinctive experience in the

Swiss Alps. It is the ideal location for a pleasant and stress-free stay thanks to its breathtaking views and contemporary conveniences.

13. Hotel de la Couronne

In the center of Paris, there is a stylish boutique hotel called Hotel de la Couronne. It provides a special fusion of contemporary conveniences and old-world charm. You are welcomed by elegant design and first-rate service as soon as you enter the foyer. The hotel offers a selection of rooms and suites, all of which have contemporary conveniences including air conditioning, flat-screen TVs, and free Wi-Fi.

The restaurant and bar in the hotel are great places to unwind after a long day. The menu features a variety of dishes from both foreign and traditional French cuisine. To accommodate all preferences, the bar provides a variety of wines, spirits, and cocktails.

The hotel provides a variety of packages and special deals for customers seeking a bit extra luxury. Visitors may take advantage of a soothing massage, a personal city tour, or even a private supper for two.

The hotel's rates fluctuate according to the time of year, but a regular room normally costs between €100 and €250 per night. The hotel also provides suites, which start at €300 per night for customers seeking a more opulent stay. Whatever kind of stay you like, Hotel de la Couronne will undoubtedly make it comfortable and pleasurable for you.

14. Hotel Center

In the center of the city, Hotel Center is a contemporary hotel. With its cutting-edge design, roomy accommodations, and practical conveniences, it offers its visitors a wonderful experience. Flat-screen TVs, free Wi-Fi, and contemporary appliances are all included in the accommodations. Each morning, a free breakfast buffet is available to guests.

The hotel provides a range of options, from short-term visits to extended stays. Prices vary based on the package type selected, however, they are often reasonable. The cost each night for visitors may range from $50 to $200. All year long, the hotel also provides special discounts and promotions.

Travelers seeking an economical but nice lodging option can go to Hotel Center. It's a great option for every tourist because of its handy location and first-rate facilities.

15. Hôtel Le Royal

A five-star luxury hotel called Hôtel Le Royal is located in the heart of Paris. It offers luxurious, contemporary lodging with cityscape views. A restaurant, bar, front desk open around-the-clock, fitness center, and sauna are just a few of the facilities available to visitors.

To meet varied demands, the hotel provides a range of accommodations kinds. All of the available rooms—standard, deluxe, and suite—are furnished with contemporary amenities. There is soundproofing, air conditioning, free Wi-Fi, a private bathroom, and sitting space in every room. Some rooms additionally include a balcony or patio with city views.

A variety of services are provided by the hotel to make sure visitors have a comfortable and happy stay. A concierge, room service, and laundry are a few of them. On-site amenities include a business center and conference rooms.

Hôtel Le Royal has reasonable rates per night. Standard rooms cost €190 per night, while deluxe rooms start at €250 and suites cost €350. Seasonal variations in prices are possible.

16. Ibis Budget Luxembourg Sud

Modern and very affordable, Ibis Budget Luxembourg Sud is located in the center of Luxembourg. The hotel's convenient location in the city's center makes it the ideal starting point for exploring this exciting area. It's the ideal spot to stay while visiting Luxembourg because of the large and comfortable accommodations, first-rate amenities, and fantastic location.

From single rooms to family rooms, the hotel provides a range of accommodations, all of which come with the newest conveniences. The hotel has free WiFi, and the front desk is open around-the-clock to assist with any questions.

Every morning at the hotel's breakfast room, a delectable buffet breakfast is also provided. The 24-hour vending machines provide a variety of food and beverages to guests as well.

Those seeking a cheap hotel in Luxembourg might choose Ibis Budget Luxembourg Sud. This hotel is a wonderful choice for individuals on a tight budget since rates start at only €50 per night.

17. Hotel La Metairie

In the center of Paris stands the opulent 4-star Hotel La Metairie. Travelers may make use of the hotel's many facilities, which include a heated indoor pool, a cutting-edge fitness center, and a spa. The hotel also provides a range of dining alternatives, including both foreign and traditional French cuisine.

The cost of the hotel varies based on the kind of accommodation and the time of booking. A normal double room may cost between €160 and €270 per night, while a deluxe double room can cost between €195 and €320. The hotel also provides several packages, including family, honeymoon, and business-related packages.

In addition, Hotel La Metairie has complimentary parking, Wi-Fi, a 24-hour front desk, and laundry facilities. The Eiffel Tower and the Louvre are just a few of the city's attractions that are near the hotel.

Hotel La Metairie is the ideal option whether you're seeking a luxurious break or a place to relax while traveling for work. This hotel will provide visitors with an amazing experience thanks to its opulent facilities and affordable rates.

18. Hotel-Restaurant A Sonnenhof

In the center of the Swiss Alps, there lies a family-run hotel called Hotel Restaurant A Sonnenhof. It has a warm, inviting ambiance with wonderful views of the mountains in the area. The hotel's accessible location makes it the ideal starting point for exploring the region's attractions.

The hotel has a range of accommodations, including single, double, and suite rooms, all of which come with contemporary conveniences. Additionally, some rooms have balconies with mountain views. The on-site restaurant offers a variety of foreign meals in addition to contemporary and traditional Swiss fare. At the bar, visitors may also savor a selection of beverages and food.

Additionally, the hotel has a fitness center, free parking, and free WiFi. For visitors' enjoyment, the hotel provides a range of activities and excursions.

The cost of a single room at Hotel Restaurant A Sonnenhof is €80 per night, while a double room is €130 per night. All year long, there are special promotions available.

19. Hotel Restaurant La Fayette

A lovely hotel called Hotel Restaurant La Fayette is situated on the outskirts of Bordeaux, a historic French city. The hotel provides a selection of opulent lodging options, from traditional rooms to suites, all with cutting-edge facilities and first-rate service. The hotel's restaurant serves delectable French-inspired cuisine that includes regional delicacies and fine wines. In addition, the hotel offers a variety of activities, including shopping, sightseeing, and sports like golf and cycling.

With rooms starting at around €85 per night, Hotel Restaurant La Fayette's nightly rates are relatively affordable. The Romance Package, which includes a bottle of sparkling wine, a bouquet, and supper at the hotel restaurant, is just one of the many packages available to guests to fit their budget and interests. A two-night stay in a Deluxe Suite, breakfast, and supper for two at the hotel restaurant are included in the Deluxe Suite Package, which provides an even more opulent experience.

With its great service and affordable costs, Hotel Restaurant La Fayette is guaranteed to provide a wonderful experience whether you're planning a romantic break or a business trip.

20. Hotel du Commerce

For those seeking a premium stay in the center of Paris, Hotel du Commerce is a perfect choice. The hotel's location in the 9th arrondissement provides easy access to some of the city's most well-known landmarks, such as the Eiffel Tower, the Louvre, and the Champs-Elysees. The hotel provides a selection of elegantly furnished rooms and suites with contemporary furnishings and conveniences. Free Wi-Fi, a fitness facility, and a round-the-clock concierge service are available to guests.

The Hotel du Commerce has a variety of price alternatives to accommodate various spending limits. Deluxe suites may go up to €300 per night, while basic rooms start at €120. A special discount is offered to those who make reservations in advance. Additionally, the hotel provides a variety of promos and packages, such as weekend getaways and family savings.

Hotel du Commerce can guarantee a memorable stay, whether you're planning a business trip or a romantic break. It's the ideal location to experience Paris because of its easy access to top attractions, opulent facilities, and affordable rates.

WHAT TO DO IN LUXEMBOURG

The little European nation of Luxembourg has a lot to offer tourists in terms of activities and sights to visit. Luxembourg is a hidden gem that should be on the radar of any traveler seeking an unforgettable experience because of its beautiful landscape, incredible architecture, vibrant culture, and top-notch cuisine.

Luxembourg has a wide range of outdoor sports for the daring. Visitors can go hiking, biking, and kayaking while exploring the Ardennes region's rolling hills and lush valleys. In the winter, there are several options for skiing and snowboarding. Additionally, year-round hot air balloon rides are offered for those seeking a distinctive perspective of the nation.

The city of Luxembourg is home to a variety of museums, galleries, and theaters for those with an interest in the arts. A must-see is the Grand Ducal Palace, one of the city's most spectacular structures. It provides guided tours and is the location of the State Art Collection. With its extensive collection of artwork, artifacts, and decorative items from all over the world, the National Museum of History and Art is also worth a visit.

Luxembourg has a lot to offer those seeking a gastronomic adventure. There are several Michelin-starred restaurants in the city, but you should also check out the neighborhood restaurants. Luxembourg's cuisine is distinct and varied, influenced by a blend of French, German, and Belgian flavors. Make sure to try regional dishes like "Bouneschlupp" and "Gromperekichelchen" (potato pancakes) (green bean soup).

A visit to some of Luxembourg's vineyards is a must for any vacation there. Some of the top wineries in the nation and some of the world's finest wines may be found in the Moselle Valley. The city of Echternach is an excellent spot to enjoy the regional delicacy "Spritzbredele," a sort of spiced biscuit. This will give you a taste of something more distinctive.

Luxembourg offers experiences for everyone, whether they are seeking outdoor adventure, cultural encounters, or a distinctive gastronomic excursion. This little nation is a fantastic choice for any visitor searching for a unique experience because of its fascinating history, breathtaking scenery, and dynamic culture.

I recently had the pleasure of traveling to Luxembourg and had an amazing experience. I found a wide variety of things to do, from hiking in the breathtaking Ardennes area to trying the unique food in the city of Luxembourg.

I began my journey by seeing the Moselle Valley's vineyards. I went to some of the greatest vineyards in the nation and sampled some strange wines there. I then continued to the city of Luxembourg where I spent some time seeing its theaters, art galleries, and museums. The Grand Ducal Palace, which houses the State Art Collection and provides guided tours, was where I spent a day.

I also got to sample some of the city's regional food. I tried foods like "Bouneschlupp" and "Gromperekichelchen," which are potato pancakes (green bean soup). I even sampled the regional delicacy, a kind of spicy cookie called "Spritzbredele." The variety of tastes and the quality of the ingredients astounded me.

Finally, I went hiking, biking, and kayaking in the magnificent Ardennes area. I was also able to go on a hot air balloon journey, which provided me with a fascinating perspective of the breathtaking scenery.

Overall, I had an incredible time on my vacation to Luxembourg. This little nation has something for everyone, from its great culture and food to its outdoor activities. I wholeheartedly advise a trip to Luxembourg if you're searching for a memorable experience.

The examples of what to do and where they are in Luxembourg are listed below.

1. Tour the Ardennes region's lovely valleys and rolling hills (Ardennes region)

2. During the winter, go skiing and snowboarding (Ardennes region)

3. Fly in a hot air balloon (Ardennes region)

4. Go to the Imperial Palace (Luxembourg city)

5. Visit the National Museum of History and Art in number five (Luxembourg city)

6. Suggest trying regional meals like "Bouneschlupp," a green bean soup, and "Gromperekichelchen," potato pancakes (Luxembourg city)

7. Tour some of the nation's top vineyards (Moselle Valley)

8. Indulge in a "Spritzbredele," a sort of spicy biscuit, a local delicacy (Echternach)

WHAT TO PACK TO LUXEMBOURG

Beautiful Luxembourg is a land rich in culture, history, and breathtaking scenery. You'll want to make sure you have everything you need as a tourist to make the most of your trip. Here is a list of what you need to bring to Luxembourg to have the greatest experience.

First and foremost, you should make sure you have a good camera and other necessary equipment because Luxembourg's breathtaking landscape and quaint cities are too lovely to ignore. To ensure that you don't miss any of the breathtaking sites, remember to pack extra memory cards and batteries.

Next, include seasonal clothing in your luggage. It's wise to be ready for anything because Luxembourg's weather may be erratic. Don't forget to pack a pair of comfortable shoes for exploring, a light coat or jacket, and warm clothing for the evenings.

A reference book is necessary for history enthusiasts. A guidebook can help you make the most of your vacation to Luxembourg, which is packed with fascinating historical sites. In addition, if you intend to visit any museums, you might want to pack a notebook to write down notes and, if you're feeling very inspired, a sketch.

Last but not least, remember to pack a few things to make you stay more pleasant. Always pack a small first-aid kit, a power adaptor, and some food in case you grow hungry while traveling.

You'll be prepared for any adventure Luxembourg has in store for you with these supplies. Enjoy the journey!

WHAT TO PACK FOR SUMMER

The summer season in Luxembourg is a fantastic experience packed with outdoor activities, cultural pursuits, and delectable cuisine. But being prepared and bringing the appropriate belongings will help you make the most of your time in the Grand Duchy. Here are some necessities to pack in your backpack, whether you're a return guest or a first-time visitor, for an unforgettable summer in Luxembourg.

You should first and foremost make sure you have a lot of sunscreen with you. In the summer, it can get rather warm in Luxembourg, and the sun can be very strong. Pack sunscreen that has an SPF of 30 or higher and is available in both lotion and spray form for simple application. Don't forget to protect yourself from the sun by wearing a hat, sunglasses, and some light clothing.

You should also make sure you have a lot of cozy, seasonally suitable apparel. Bring a range of versatile clothing items, such as shorts and T-shirts, thin long-sleeve shirts, and a couple of sweaters or light jackets for the evenings. Bring rain gear as well in case of an unexpected downpour.

It's crucial to have the appropriate footwear if you intend to enjoy the outdoors. Good socks and sturdy shoes are needed. Bring a pair of sandals or lightweight shoes if you intend to go trekking.

Finally, remember the fundamentals. Pack some personal care supplies like soap, toothpaste, and shampoo in addition to a first aid kit, a flashlight, and a map. Because Luxembourg utilizes a different kind of electrical outlet than the majority of other nations, be sure to also pack a universal adaptor.

Making the effort to pack the appropriate belongings will ensure that you are ready for any activity you might engage in while in Luxembourg. With these necessities, you'll be able to visit the nation's top sites and have a summer that will never be forgotten.

EXAMPLES:

-Sunscreen (SPF 30 or higher, lotion and spray form)

-Hat

-Sunglasses

-Light clothing

-Rain gear

-Comfortable, weather-appropriate clothing

-Sturdy shoes

-Lightweight shoes or sandals

-Toiletries (soap, toothpaste, shampoo, etc.)

-First-aid kit

-Flashlight

-Map

-Universal adapter and many more.

WHAT TO PACK FOR WINTER

With its snow-covered hills, charming towns, and fine architecture, winter in Luxembourg is a wonderful season. As a visitor, it's crucial to be outfitted for the chilly weather and ensure that your luggage is full of the appropriate materials. Here is a list of things you'll need to be warm and cozy during your winter visit to Luxembourg.

You'll need a warm coat most of all. To shield you from the elements, choose a windproof and waterproof coat. In any weather, a high-quality coat will keep you dry and toasty. Pack a scarf, hat, and gloves as well to protect your hands, neck, and head from the elements.

Boots are a need to include in your luggage. Selecting a pair that is cozy and waterproof will assist keep your feet dry and toasty during your winter trip. To keep your feet warm and dry, be sure to carry extra socks and waterproof shoe coverings.

Wear thermal layers and long underwear to keep your body warm. Choose lightweight, breathable materials that nonetheless provide enough insulation. Due to its inherent warmth and insulation, wool is a fantastic material for winter clothing.

Pack several pairs of waterproof pants and a waterproof jacket in case you encounter a snowfall or downpour. Additionally, a layer of insulation will be added by a nice pair of pants and a jacket, keeping you warm.

Last but not least, remember to include a few additional accessories. Goggles, a neck gaiter, and a thick winter cap are all useful accessories to have on hand. While you tour the city, a pair of warm winter gloves will help keep your hands warm.

You may prepare for anything the winter in Luxembourg throws at you by paying attention to this advice. You may easily enjoy your winter vacation if you bring the necessary stuff.

An example of things to bring to Luxembourg during the winter:

• Waterproof pants and jacket

• Winter coat

• Hat, scarf, and gloves

• Boots

• Long underwear and thermal layers

• Winter hat

- Goggles

- Neck gaiter

- Thick winter gloves and many more.

WHAT TO PACK FOR SPRING

Due to its well-known mild temperature, Luxembourg is the ideal place for travelers wishing to visit in the spring. However, it's crucial to take into account the varied activities offered and the unpredictable weather while preparing for a vacation to Luxembourg. What to bring for a springtime vacation to Luxembourg, from seeing the nation's ancient landmarks and castles to visiting its numerous parks and gardens.

To begin with, it's critical to prepare for erratic weather. Despite Luxembourg's reputation for moderate weather, frigid days and downpours may nevertheless happen. Pack a lightweight raincoat or waterproof jacket, as well as a scarf or shawl for extra warmth, to be ready for everything. Pack a pair of relaxed, water-resistant shoes or boots if you want to explore the countryside.

When it comes to apparel, bring your favorite, multipurpose, lightweight pieces. It should be sufficient to bring a few breathable blouses, a pair of trousers, and a few dresses or skirts. Remember to include a few layers, such as a cardigan or lightweight jacket, as well as a couple of scarves. If you want to visit some of Luxembourg's more affluent restaurants, be sure to include a couple of pairs of casual shoes, such as sneakers and sandals, as well as a pair of dressier shoes.

Don't forget to take some stuff for outdoor activities if you want to make the most of your vacation. Bring a hat, sunscreen, and sunglasses if you want to take in the views and explore Luxembourg's many parks, gardens, and monuments. Bring some snacks and a reusable water bottle so you can keep hydrated and fed while on your journey. Pack a good pair of walking shoes and a camera to capture the breathtaking vistas if you want to visit one of Luxembourg's numerous castles.

Finally, to make sure you're ready for anything, pack some essentials before you go on your vacation, such as a first-aid kit and a global power adaptor.

With the help of this packing list, you'll be prepared to visit Luxembourg in the spring and take advantage of the country's many attractions and pleasant weather. Therefore, remember to bring your favorite goods so that you may enjoy your vacation the most.

Examples Of What To Pack In Luxembourg For Spring include:

Waterproof shoes or boots, a lightweight raincoat or waterproof jacket, a scarf or shawl, lightweight blouses, dresses or skirts, a cardigan or lightweight jacket, scarves, comfortable shoes, a hat, sunscreen, sunglasses, snacks, and a reusable water bottle are all necessary outfits, a camera, a first-aid kit, a pair of sturdy walking shoes, and a universal power adapter.

CHAPTER THREE
FOODS AND DRINKS

A little yet stunning nation called Luxembourg is tucked away in the center of Europe. It is no surprise that Luxembourg draws visitors from all over the globe with its gorgeous towns, undulating hills, and unique culture. And one of the finest ways to get to know a place is via its cuisine and beverages.

In terms of cuisine, Luxembourg is a culinary paradise. The cuisines of Luxembourg are among the greatest in Europe, with delectable dishes that have been handed down through the centuries and fresh, locally sourced ingredients.

Several traditional foods are available to start, such as "Gromper Kichelcher," a potato pancake stuffed with bacon, mushrooms, onions, and spices. Or try the delectable "F'schierkraut," a meal with pork and cabbage.

Some of the world's best domestic and imported beers are available in Luxembourg. The "Cristal," a pale lager made in the nation since 1842, is a favorite among residents. The "Munner," a dark and smokey beer, is a must-try for those seeking something a little heavier.

Last but not least, no trip to Luxembourg would be complete without trying some of the local wines. The Moselle Valley is home to some of the best wines in the world, including the renowned

"Riesling." Alternatively, try the "Pinot Gris," a fruity and light white wine.

Everybody may find something they want to eat or drink in Luxembourg. The nation offers a variety of cuisines to choose from, whether you're craving something familiar or something more unique. Don't pass up the opportunity to experience some of the finest cuisine and beverages in Europe when you visit Luxembourg.

Recently, I had the pleasure of traveling to Luxembourg and trying some of the cuisine and beverages there. The classic "Gromper Kichelcher" was one of my favorite experiences. It was incredibly amazing. This potato pancake was stuffed with bacon, mushrooms, onions, and spices. I also got to sample a few of the regional brews, including the well-known "Cristal." This light, crisp pale beer was certainly worth trying. I also sampled some of the regional wines, including the delicious "Riesling" and "Pinot Gris." Overall, I had a genuinely unforgettable time with the food and beverages in Luxembourg, and I heartily suggest it to anybody searching for a fantastic culinary adventure.

RESTAURANTS

The undiscovered jewel of Europe, Luxembourg, is a wonderful place to spend a vacation. It provides something for everyone with its breathtaking scenery, rich cultural legacy, and exciting nightlife. Luxembourg is also not a slouch when it comes to cuisine. The restaurants in Luxembourg are likely to tempt your taste buds with their vivid fusion of European, French, and Italian food.

There are many different cuisines to sample at the restaurants in Luxembourg. You may find something to satiate every appetite, from traditional Luxembourgish food like Friture de la Moselle to more French-inspired fare like Quiche Lorraine and Croque Monsieur. A range of exotic cuisines, including Indian, Chinese, and even Mexican, are also available. Whatever your taste, you can find something to satisfy it.

The distinctive atmosphere of the restaurants in Luxembourg is certainly likely to wow. A lot of the restaurants are situated in charming, inviting structures with a touch of grandeur. The menus are often thoughtfully designed to suit every taste, and the staff is polite and educated. The chefs are renowned for their cutting-edge methods, and several of the restaurants have even received Michelin stars.

The outstanding service at Luxembourg's restaurants is likewise well-known. You will be given a warm welcome as soon as you enter, and the staff will make every effort to make your visit enjoyable. No matter whether you're planning a family reunion or a romantic evening for two, Luxembourg's restaurants will make your meal special.

There is something for every palette in Luxembourg, which is home to some of Europe's top eateries. The restaurants in Luxembourg will provide a distinctive and remarkable experience, whether you're seeking a typical Luxembourgish dinner or something more experimental. Check out the restaurants in Luxembourg if you want to have a wonderful vacation.

Here Includes the Restaurant Name And Addresses

1. L'Ours Restaurant in Luxembourg City

2. EKiSS, Esch-sur-Alzette

3. Wiltz, La Table

4. Esch-sur-La Alzette's Pomme d'Or

5. La Brasserie in Luxembourg City,

6. Le Vivarais and Mersch

7. Luxembourg City's L'Essentiel

8. The Old Inn in Ettelbruck

9. Le Relais in Luxembourg City

10. Luxembourg City's La Belle Vie

How much do they cost?

Depending on the cuisine and ambiance you like, restaurants in Luxembourg range widely in price. For instance, depending on the items you choose, a supper at L'Ours in Luxembourg City might cost anywhere from €25 and €80 per person. A three-course lunch at La Table in Wiltz is more affordable, costing between $20 and $30. On the opposite end of the range, you may discover eateries with superb menus and rates per person ranging from €50 to €100, as La Pomme d'Or in Esch-sur-Alzette.

The quality and service of the restaurants in Luxembourg that I recently had the pleasure of visiting left me pleased. All of the eateries I went to had mouthwatering food with a variety of taste options. The environment was warm and welcoming, and the personnel was kind and helpful. Anyone searching for a unique dining experience should check out the eateries in Luxembourg.

BARS AND PUBS

The vibrant nightlife in Luxembourg gives tourists the chance to explore a variety of clubs and pubs in the heart of Europe. Luxembourg has something for everyone to enjoy, from the charming and intimate to the colorful and high-energy. There is certain to be a bar or pub that will suit your requirements, whether you're searching for a romantic evening out with your significant other, a crazy night of partying with friends, or just a calm evening to take in the sights and sounds of the city.

Luxembourg's taverns and pubs provide a distinctive fusion of atmosphere and culture. The city is home to many old English-style pubs, like The Old Duke and The Fox & Hounds, for guests seeking a traditional pub experience. Here, you may unwind with a delicious meal and a pint of locally-made beer in a welcoming setting. For those seeking a little more opulence, Luxembourg also has a wide selection of stylish and contemporary clubs and bars, including the well-known Bar des Caves, which offers a choice of artisan cocktails and tapas.

Luxembourg undoubtedly has plenty to offer, regardless of the style of bar or pub experience you're seeking. It's simple to locate a place to fit your interests in Luxembourg since so many clubs and pubs have live music. There are several locations in the city where you can unwind, enjoy some excellent music, and have a few drinks, from jazz and blues to rock and reggae.

A terrific spot to meet residents and tourists alike is in Luxembourg's taverns and pubs. It's simple to meet friends and have enjoyable talks with people from various walks of life in the city because of its well-known laid-back and inviting vibe. The bars and pubs in Luxembourg will undoubtedly provide a distinctive experience, whether you're trying to meet new people or just enjoy a drink in a welcoming environment.

Both visitors and residents may enjoy Luxembourg's bars and pubs, which range from quaint taverns to stylish lounges. There is bound to be a bar or pub in Luxembourg that will meet your requirements, whether you're searching for a quiet evening for two or a crazy night out with friends. Luxembourg is the ideal location for a night out in the heart of Europe because of its lively environment and inviting vibe.

Notable bars and pubs in Luxembourg together with their addresses.

1. The Old Duke at Luxembourg City's Grand Rue

2. The Fox & Hounds on Luxembourg City's Place Guillaume II

3. Bar des Caves on Luxembourg City's Place Guillaume II

4. The Jazz Café at Luxembourg City's Place d'Armes

5. The Blue Note at Luxembourg City's Place des Bains

6. The Wunderbar at Luxembourg City's Rue de Strasbourg

7. The Great Escape, Luxembourg City's Rue de l'Alzette

8. The Globe at Luxembourg City's Place Clairefontaine

9. The Back Room, Luxembourg City's Place d'Armes

10. The Living Room at Luxembourg City's Rue de Neudorf

How Much Does Travel To These Bars And Pubs Cost?

The price to go to a bar or a pub in Luxembourg varies based on the kind of establishment, the beverages you buy, and other elements. In Luxembourg, a beer or glass of wine typically costs between €4 and €7, while the price of a cocktail or mixed drink might vary from €7 to €15.

I had a great day exploring Luxembourg's taverns and pubs. Each pub had a friendly, inviting environment, and the beverages were moderately priced. The staff was helpful and pleasant, and they were always glad to assist me in selecting the ideal beverage. Some of the establishments included live music, which I liked since it created a distinctive and exciting ambiance. Overall, I had a fantastic day exploring Luxembourg's bars and pubs, and I'd heartily suggest them to anybody seeking a fun night out.

CHAPTER FOUR

SHOPPING AND MALL

Despite being a little nation buried away in the middle of Europe, Luxembourg has a lot to offer in terms of mall experiences and shopping. For anyone wishing to indulge in some retail therapy, Luxembourg is a fantastic trip. It has everything from famous worldwide boutiques and department stores to stylish local designer shops.

The capital city of Luxembourg City, which is home to some of the nation's top malls and retail complexes, is at the core of the country's shopping scene. The biggest of them is the vast Auchan Luxembourg Shopping Complex, which has more than 100 shops, eateries, and entertainment facilities. From designer goods and high-end clothing to local and worldwide names, customers can find it all here. The center is a terrific spot to spend the day since it has a big food court and a movie theater.

The City Concorde, which is a well-liked shopping center in Luxembourg City, is close to the main plaza. This mall features a huge selection of shops, from high-end labels to more budget-friendly businesses, as well as a range of eateries and cafés. The mall is a terrific spot to spend the day with family and friends since it also has a bowling alley and an ice skating rink.

Luxembourg has a variety of smaller, independent shops and boutiques for those seeking a more boutique shopping experience.

Some of Luxembourg's most distinctive establishments, including art galleries, artisanal craft stores, and antique shops, may be found in the Grund neighborhood of the capital city. Together with many other upscale retailers, the "rue de la Boucherie" is home to Chanel and Gucci.

Lastly, Luxembourg is home to a variety of historic markets, like the "Marche des Fleurs" in Luxembourg City and the weekly markets in the villages of Echternach and Grevenmacher, for those seeking a more traditional shopping experience. These markets provide a fantastic opportunity to purchase homemade handicrafts, fresh fruit, and local mementos.

Luxembourg offers plenty to offer everyone, regardless of the kind of shopping experience they're searching for. Luxembourg is a terrific destination for all sorts of consumers, offering everything from world-class malls and department shops to local markets and small boutiques.

Examples Of Shopping And Mall

The Grund neighborhood of Luxembourg City, the City Concorde, the Auchan Luxembourg Shopping Center, the Marche des Fleurs, the Echternach and Grevenmacher weekly markets, and more

I recently had a weekend trip to Luxembourg and was pleasantly impressed by the caliber of the retail opportunities on offer. There was something for everyone, from upscale shops in the city to old-fashioned markets in the countryside. I had a lot of fun visiting Luxembourg City's Grund neighborhood, which was packed with distinctive shops and art galleries. With its extensive selection of stores and entertainment options, the Auchan Shopping Centre was a fantastic spot to spend the day. I had a great day in Luxembourg overall and was pleasantly pleased by the range of shopping options.

I bought several trinkets from the neighborhood markets, such as handcrafted ceramics, and jewelry. A set of earrings from a regional jewelry artist was one of the designer items I purchased from a couple of the shops in the Grund neighborhood. Last but not least, I made a few purchases in the Auchan Shopping Center, including a new outfit and some cosmetics.

Depending on the retailer and the item, the pricing of the things I bought in Luxembourg varied. I spent between 10 and 30 euros on handcrafted jewelry and ceramics in the neighborhood markets. The prices of the designer items from the Grund neighborhood ranged from 50 to 100 euros. The products I bought at the Auchan Shopping Centre were the priciest, costing between 100 and 200 euros.

Finally, I'd suggest people benefit from the distinctive shopping opportunities Luxembourg has to offer. There are many places to look for one-of-a-kind goods and souvenirs, from trendy shops in the city to old-fashioned markets in the countryside. I'd advise purchasing some locally created jewelry or ceramics from the markets as well as some high-end stuff from the Grund neighborhood. The Auchan Shopping Centre also offers a large range of goods, including electronics, household goods, and things for fashion and cosmetics.

MARKET IN LUXEMBOURG

For travelers seeking a memorable and thrilling experience, Luxembourg is a charming and bustling location. Luxembourg has something for everyone, whether you want to experience its magnificent architecture, delve into its fascinating history, or indulge in its delectable food. The vibrant markets in Luxembourg are one of the pleasures of any vacation there.

The markets in Luxembourg are a destination unto themselves and are a riot of activity, color, and culture. The markets in Luxembourg provide everything you might want, including fresh food, handmade items, traditional apparel, and souvenirs. The Kirchberg Market, which takes place every Saturday in the city's old town, is the most well-known market in Luxembourg. Anything from fruits and vegetables to clothing, artwork, and toys may be found here for tourists.

The Walferdange Market, held every Sunday in the lovely park of the city, is another well-liked market. This market is particularly well-known for its great street food, traditional crafts, and apparel.

The markets in Luxembourg are fantastic places to learn about the traditions and culture of the nation. The markets provide a peek into the life of the locals of Luxembourg, from performances of native music and dance to the pleasant chatter of the merchants.

The markets in Luxembourg are an essential must-visit, whether you're searching for a one-of-a-kind shopping experience or simply a fun day out. They will undoubtedly be a highlight of your journey to this beautiful nation since they have something for everyone.

The market in Luxembourg was a fantastic experience for me. I was able to locate a broad variety of goods from regional merchants, including handmade goods and fresh fruit. I loved seeing the traditional crafts and attire on exhibit, and the atmosphere was bright and vivid. I enjoyed sampling the delectable street food. That was a fantastic chance to learn more about the nation's culture and traditions.

The Kirchberg Market, held in the city's historic district every Saturday, and the Walferdange Market, held in the city's lovely park every Sunday, are the two most well-liked markets in Luxembourg. The Vianden Market in the town of Vianden, the Esch-sur-Sûre Market in the hamlet of Esch-sur-Sûre, and the Ettelbruck Market in the city of Ettelbruck are just a few of the country's smaller marketplaces.

Depending on what you buy, shopping in the markets in Luxembourg might become expensive. Although traditional attire and fresh fruit are often relatively reasonable, souvenirs and artisan products may be significantly more costly. The markets are still a fantastic deal, however, since a large variety of goods can be found there at affordable prices.

Anybody traveling to Luxembourg should make sure to visit the markets, in my opinion. They provide a wonderful opportunity to discover some interesting goods at discount rates while also getting a taste of the local way of life. Although many businesses may not take credit cards, be sure to have cash. Most essential, remember to enjoy yourself.

SHOPPING DISTRICTS IN LUXEMBOURG

The city of Luxembourg is a thriving, busy hub of trade and culture, and this is also true of its retail sector. As a visitor, you'll be surrounded by upscale boutiques and global department stores that sell a wide selection of luxury products and high-end designer goods. Luxembourg's retail area provides something for everyone, whether you're seeking the newest styles or a vintage favorite.

The Grand Rue, Luxembourg's major shopping avenue, is dotted with upscale shops, high-end retailers, and name-brand clothing stores. Anything from designer apparel and accessories to one-of-a-kind jewelry and home goods may be found here. Check the pricing before purchasing many of the shops provide discounts.

The Place d'Armes is a beautiful area with cafés and restaurants located just off the Grand Rue. This is the ideal location to have a meal or a cup of coffee away from the bustle of the retail center. Locals and visitors alike use the area in the summer to take in the ambiance and the sun.

Another well-liked retail district with a variety of stores is Avenue de la Liberté. A variety of local shops and international designer labels may be found here. You may select from a variety of restaurants and cafés to get a bite to eat while you browse.

Without stopping through the Auchan Shopping Center, no trip to Luxembourg's retail sector would be complete. Many worldwide brands and retailers, as well as a wide range of eateries, cafés, and bars, can be found at this sizable shopping mall. There are other entertainment alternatives including a movie theater and a bowling facility.

Tourists seeking a distinctive shopping experience will find Luxembourg's retail area to be a dream location. There is something for everyone with its upscale shops, department stores, and designer brands. Luxembourg's retail area provides something for everyone, regardless of whether you're seeking the newest styles or a timeless classic.

Luxembourg Shopping District Examples

The major shopping district of Luxembourg is called Grand Rue, and it is dotted with upscale shops, chain stores, and high-end brands.

Place d'Armes: This quaint area, which is surrounded by cafés and restaurants, is the ideal spot to escape the bustle of the retail district.

Avenue de la Liberté: This street has a wide selection of stores and boutiques in addition to a large number of cafés and eateries.

Many worldwide brands and retailers, as well as a wide assortment of eateries, cafés, and bars, can be found in the Auchan Shopping Center.

Luxurious items and designer brands are available at a range of shops and boutiques in Luxembourg's lively shopping center. Everyone may find something in Luxembourg's retail area, which offers everything from high-end fashion shops to department stores and distinctive jewelry.

The Grand Rue, Luxembourg's major shopping avenue, is dotted with upscale shops, chain businesses, and designer brands. Here, you may discover both the newest fashions and time-tested classics. Also, a lot of the shops have sales, so it pays to compare costs before making a purchase.

A respite from shopping is ideal in the picturesque Plaza d'Armes, a square brimming with cafés and eateries. Locals and visitors alike use the area in the summer to take in the ambiance and the sun.

Another well-liked shopping district is the Avenue de la Liberté, which has a wide selection of stores and boutiques in addition to a large number of cafés and eateries.

The Auchan Shopping Center, a sizable shopping complex, is also home to a wide range of eateries, cafés, and bars in addition to a great selection of international brands and retailers. There are other entertainment alternatives including a movie theater and a bowling facility.

Thus, Luxembourg's retail area is the ideal place to go if you're seeking a distinctive shopping experience. Luxembourg's retail area provides something for everyone, regardless of whether you're seeking the newest styles or a timeless classic.

I would advise anybody visiting Luxembourg's retail district to look around and take advantage of all the many shops and boutiques. There are many different types of retailers in Luxembourg, from department stores to specialty jewelry shops to high-end designer boutiques. When making a purchase, be careful to compare pricing since many of the shops have sales.

Spend some time exploring the nearby cafés and eateries as well. A respite from shopping is ideal in the picturesque Plaza d'Armes, a square brimming with cafés and eateries. Also, there are several restaurants, cafés, and bars as well as a movie theater, bowling alley, and other entertainment venues within the Auchan Shopping Complex.

Finally, remember to check out the nearby boutiques and shops if you're looking for something a little more distinctive. Local shops and international designer labels are mixed in this area to give a wide selection of unusual goods.

So, I would advise anybody visiting Luxembourg's retail district to take advantage of the area's many shops and establishments by exploring it. Enjoy your stay in the city and stop by the cafés and restaurants to relax after a long day of shopping.

CHAPTER FIVE

ENTERTAINMENT

One of Europe's most stunning nations, Luxembourg is a popular travel destination for travelers interested in the incredible culture and entertainment it has to offer. Luxembourg has a wide variety of leisure options for people of all ages and interests, from its beautiful towns and countryside to its varied geography and culture.

With a wide variety of bars, clubs, and pubs, Luxembourg provides a thriving nightlife for anyone wishing to have a fun night out. There is something for everyone, from hip cocktail bars in the city to live music venues in the countryside. Also, visitors may savor a range of classic and contemporary foods, such as French, Italian, German, and even Belgian fare. There are also many theaters, movie theaters, and other entertainment places where you may see everything from musicals to comedies.

Luxembourg offers a wide range of family-friendly attractions and outdoor activities for individuals who like being outside. There is something for everyone, from the renowned Moselle Valley to the Ardennes mountain range. Tourists may enjoy water sports, relax on the beaches, and explore the breathtaking landscapes and woodlands. Children may engage in a variety of activities, including visiting aquariums, zoos, and amusement parks.

Luxembourg is home to several fascinating museums and monuments for individuals who have a love for history and culture. Visitors may discover more about the history and culture of the nation at places like the Grand Ducal Palace and the Luxembourg City Museum. The Summer in the City Festival, which honors Luxembourg's musical tradition, is only one of the many festivals and events that take place all year long.

Luxembourg has something to suit every interest. For those eager to have a good time, there is no lack of entertainment, from its thriving nightlife and culture to its breathtaking scenery and sights. So why not book your vacation to this wonderful nation and take advantage of all Luxembourg has to offer?

A trip to Luxembourg is a once-in-a-lifetime adventure. Everyone may enjoy the region's breathtaking scenery, colorful culture, and family-friendly activities. The nation is home to several museums, monuments, festivals, and natural wonders including the world-famous Moselle Valley and Ardennes mountain range. Tourists may enjoy water sports, relax on the beaches, and explore the breathtaking countryside and woodlands.

Cities are also interesting to explore. Visitors may take part in a variety of activities and attractions in a variety of locations, from the vibrant capital city of Luxembourg City to the charming villages of the Moselle Valley. Together with theaters and movies, there are a wide variety of eateries, pubs, and clubs. Together with its many museums and monuments, the city's history and culture may all be explored by tourists.

Everyone may enjoy themselves when visiting Luxembourg, which is a wonderful location. There are several activities and sights to suit all interests, whether you want to explore the breathtaking countryside or the thriving metropolis. So why not book your vacation to Luxembourg and take advantage of all that wonderful nation has to offer?

NIGHTLIFE

Although Luxembourg is one of the most underappreciated nations in Europe, its nightlife scene is a gem just waiting to be found. The nightlife in Luxembourg is diverse and exciting, with everything from cozy pubs to exciting clubs. There is something for everyone in Luxembourg, whether you want to have a quiet evening out or a wild night of partying.

The pubs and bars in Luxembourg are the ideal starting point for anyone looking for a low-key night out. The nation is renowned for its extensive beer selection, and you can enjoy cozy settings to sample distinctive regional brews. Visit some of the city's wine bars for a more upscale setting where you can savor fine wines while listening to live music.

The clubs in Luxembourg will provide an exciting night out if that's what you're after. Luxembourg has it all, from cutting-edge EDM clubs to subterranean techno venues. Some of Europe's top DJs call the city home, and its numerous dance halls offer some truly spectacular nights.

Luxembourg boasts a variety of nightlife options, no matter what you're looking for. The nightlife in Luxembourg is likely to leave you with lifelong memories, from quaint taverns to crazy clubs. So come to Luxembourg and take in the pulsating nightlife if you don't want to miss out on this undiscovered jewel of a nation!

I just had the chance to explore Luxembourg's nightlife, and it was a wonderful experience. The city offers a wide variety of bars and pubs, from quaint taverns to posh wine bars. I enjoyed being able to try the regional wines and beers while live music played in the background.

The nightlife in Luxembourg was spectacular. I felt as though I was in another world whether I was in modern EDM clubs or underground techno venues. The atmosphere was electric, and the DJs were some of the best I've ever heard. I will most likely return soon to relive the entire experience.

Overall, I had a fantastic time experiencing Luxembourg's nightlife. I had a nice night because the city has a wide variety of bars and clubs. I would strongly advise visiting Luxembourg if you want a distinctive nightlife experience.

Although Luxembourg has a diverse nightlife, the city's core is home to some of the most well-known venues. There are several pubs, taverns, and clubs in the vicinity of Place d'Armes. The Grund neighborhood is a terrific spot to go if you want a more laid-back vibe because there are so many quaint bars and eateries there. The Glacis neighborhood, the Gare district, and the Pfaffenthal region are some more fantastic nightlife areas in Luxembourg.

Yeah, it is normally safe to explore Luxembourg at night. The streets are often well-lit and monitored, and there is little crime in the city. But, it's best to remain vigilant and aware of your surroundings at all times, just as in any city. Avoid going on a nighttime walk alone, and be careful with your belongings. You should be able to have a fun and safe night out in Luxembourg with a little prudence.

If you're thinking about visiting Luxembourg, I suggest doing some research on the best sites to visit beforehand. Examine internet evaluations, seek advice from the locals, and educate yourself about the city's nightlife. You can be sure to choose the ideal location for your particular likes in this way. I also advise taking extra security precautions, such as remaining in well-lit places and avoiding nighttime solo walks. You ought to be able to have a safe and enjoyable experience in Luxembourg with a little planning.

MUSIC

The small nation of Luxembourg is in the center of Western Europe but is not frequently considered a travel destination. However, Luxembourg has a thriving and distinctive music scene that is worth checking out. Since ancient times, music has been an integral part of Luxembourg's culture and has greatly influenced its growth.

Traditional folk music is just one of the many musical genres that are prevalent in Luxembourg.

Traditional folk instruments like the accordion, violin, and guitar are used to perform traditional folk music. In all parts of the nation, these instruments are frequently used during regional festivals and celebrations. Many of these events, including the "Rhenish" and the "Wine Festival," offer locals and visitors the chance to listen to and enjoy traditional musical genres.

The modern music scene in Luxembourg is also thriving, with both national and international artists performing there. Numerous music festivals in the nation, including Rock-A-Field, the V-Festival, and the Luxembourg Jazz Festival, draw tens of thousands of tourists each year. Numerous of them host concerts and performances by some of the biggest names in the music industry. The nation also has some of the best music venues in all of Europe.

The emphasis on education is also very strong in Luxembourg's music scene. Several prestigious music schools in the nation provide programs and courses to both domestic and foreign students, including the Conservatoire de Luxembourg and the Centre de Formation Musicale. These institutions give students the chance to learn and hone their musical abilities while also giving them the chance to interact with and meet musicians from all over the world.

The music scene in Luxembourg offers tourists a singular and unforgettable experience. Luxembourg offers something for everyone, whether you want to take advantage of the nation's music schools, attend a contemporary music festival, or experience traditional folk music. Thus, keep Luxembourg on your list the next time you're choosing a holiday spot because you won't be dissatisfied.

the best music to listen to while visiting Luxembourg

1. Customary Folk Music

2. Jazz

3. Rock

4. Pop

5. Electronic

5. Electronic

7. Traditional

8. Blues

9. Hip-Hop/Rap

10. Reggae

I had the pleasure of discovering Luxembourg's music scene while visiting the country. The variety of musical genres and styles in this nation astounded me. There was music for everyone, ranging from contemporary rock and pop to traditional folk music. The live performances were great, and the music venues were some of the best I've ever been to. The music schools in Luxembourg, which provide courses and programs to both local and foreign students, also made a lasting impression on me. Overall, I spent a wonderful day listening to the music in

Luxembourg, and I heartily endorse it to anyone seeking a special and memorable experience.

I'd advise anyone visiting Luxembourg to take advantage of the vibrant music scene there. There is something for everyone, whether you want to listen to traditional folk music, go to a contemporary music festival, or enroll in a course at one of the esteemed music schools in the nation. Spend as much time as possible in Luxembourg and immerse yourself in the country's unique music scene.

Luxembourg has a thriving and varied jazz scene, with numerous venues and events all year long. A variety of international and local jazz musicians perform at one of the biggest and most well-liked festivals, the Luxembourg Jazz Festival. The Jazz Club and the Jazz à l'Ecluse are two additional well-liked locations. For those interested in learning more about the genre, Luxembourg also offers a variety of jazz schools and courses. Overall, Luxembourg is a great choice for jazz lovers looking to take in the genre in a distinctive and lively environment.

The alternative music scene is also thriving in Luxembourg, and there are many different venues and events held there all year long. The Kulturfabrik and the Melusina are well-liked venues that frequently host concerts and events with both regional and international alternative acts. Another well-liked occasion is the Rock-A-Field festival, which offers a wonderful chance to explore Luxembourg's alternative music scene.

Luxembourg is a great place to go if you want to learn more about alternative music or if you just want to experience it live.

A thriving classical and blues music scene exists in Luxembourg as well. One of the best music schools in the nation, the Conservatoire de Luxembourg offers courses and programs to both domestic and foreign students. The Luxembourg Philharmonic Orchestra, which gives classical music performances all year round, is also housed inside the institution. The Luxembourg Blues Festival and the blues nights at the Kulturfabrik are only a couple of the places and events in Luxembourg where one may listen to blues music. Overall, Luxembourg is a fantastic place to visit if you like to listen to classical and blues music.

A flourishing pop and electronic music culture exist in Luxembourg as well. The Kulturfabrik and the Melusina are two well-liked venues that each offer a variety of regional and international performances. Thousands of people attend the V-Festival, another well-liked occasion, each year. The Club 88 and the Lux Club are only two of the electronic music-focused bars and clubs in Luxembourg. Overall, Luxembourg is a fantastic choice for travelers interested in listening to pop and techno music in a lively environment.

FESTIVAL

An annual celebration of the greatest in global cinema, the Festival International du Film de Luxembourg offers a venue for filmmakers from all over the globe to present their work. The festival, which takes place in the tiny European country of Luxembourg, has been going since 1972 and is still regarded as one of the most significant occasions in the calendar of world cinema.

Several notable feature films, documentaries, shorts, and experimental works by some of the most well-known figures in the film business will be included at this year's festival. The program's highlights include several gala screenings, unique events, and master sessions with renowned directors and performers.

The festival gives filmmakers a chance to network with other experts in the field and promote their work. The festival's jury is composed of respected business leaders and international cinema critics, and the coveted Grand Prize winner receives a sizeable monetary reward.

The festival features a wide range of ancillary events in addition to movie screenings, including panel discussions, seminars, and parties. The dynamic environment offers a wonderful chance to connect with other movie buffs and learn more about the industry.

The Festival International du Film de Luxembourg is a singular event that honors cinematic accomplishments from across the globe and serves as a reminder of the ability of film to amuse, inform, and inspire. It offers a venue for budding filmmakers to display their work and for seasoned filmmakers to provide their wisdom. With its dedication to honoring the greatest in world film, the festival makes a priceless contribution to Luxembourg's larger cultural scene.

A dynamic and varied selection of festivals is held annually in Luxembourg. They include film festivals, food and drink festivals, music festivals, and cultural festivals, among many more.

The Rock-a-Field Music Festival, the Luxembourg Jazz Festival, and the Wiltz Festival are some of the music events held in Luxembourg. One of the biggest festivals in the area, Rock-a-Field showcases a wide range of national and local bands, from current pop to vintage rock. The top jazz musicians from all over the globe perform at the annual Luxembourg Jazz Festival. In the Château de Wiltz, there are performances and recitals of classical music from the 18th and 19th centuries as part of the Wiltz Festival.

The National Day, the Christmas Market, and the Festival of Lights in Luxembourg City are examples of cultural celebrations held in the country. Luxembourg's independence is commemorated on National Day with parades and street entertainment all across the city. Each year, the Old Town hosts the Christmas Market, a customary gathering where vendors offer presents, delectable food, and festive décor. The Festival of Lights is a stunning lighting show that takes place all around the city and honors the winter solstice.

The Luxembourg Beer Festival, the Wine Festival, and the Chocolate Festival are among the food and beverage events held there. An annual celebration of the nation's brewing sector, the Luxembourg Beer Festival offers samples, live music, and food vendors. Through tastings, workshops, and food pairings, the Wine Festival highlights Luxembourg's top winemakers. The Chocolate Festival features live cooking demonstrations, seminars, and tastings to honor Luxembourg's artisanal chocolatiers.

The European Film Festival, Luxembourg City Film Festival, and Festival International du Film de Luxembourg are some of the film festivals held in Luxembourg. A selection of feature films, documentaries, short films, and experimental works by some of the most well-known figures in the film business are shown at the Festival International du Film de Luxembourg, an annual celebration of the finest in world cinema. Through screenings, panels, and prizes, the Luxembourg City Film Festival honors independent films from all around the globe. The European Film Festival is a yearly celebration of the cinematic accomplishments of the continent, including showings of the newest European movies.

Festivals in Luxembourg take place at various times and places, depending on the occasion. In June, Roeser hosts the annual Rock-a-Field music festival. Throughout the first week of July, the Place Guillaume II in Luxembourg City hosts the Luxembourg Jazz Festival. The Château de Wiltz hosts the Wiltz Festival in July and August. On June 23, National Day is celebrated in some cities across the nation. In the Old Town, the Christmas Market is held each December. December sees the Festival of Lights in Luxembourg City. The Plaza d'Armes hosts the Luxembourg Beer Festival in March. The Vinorama Wine Museum hosts the Wine Festival in May. The Old Town hosts the Chocolate Festival in November. In

April, Luxembourg City hosts the Festival International du Film de Luxembourg. The Luxembourg City Film Festival takes place in March at several locations around the city. It takes place in Luxembourg City in July for the European Film Festival.

In 2019, I had the pleasure of going to the Luxembourg International Film Festival. Being surrounded by so many ardent filmmakers and movie fans was an amazing experience. The festival itself was well run and gave filmmakers a fantastic platform to display their work. I had the chance to go to a range of screenings, discussions, and workshops, as well as get to know some of the industry insiders and film critics who were there. Hearing their observations and viewpoints on the movies being screened was motivating.

Additionally, the festival had a great vibe, with bars, cafes, and food stands serving as a lovely backdrop to the entire event. Anyone looking for a different way to watch movies should go to the festival; it was a truly memorable experience.

I would advise first-time attendees of the Festival International du Film de Luxembourg to look over the entire schedule and make a schedule in advance. Looking through the schedule of movies and choosing a handful you want to watch is a terrific idea. Also, it's critical to be informed of the showing dates and times since there may be fierce competition for seats. Planning some extra activities around the event, such as going to lectures, going to bars and cafés, or seeing the city, is also a wonderful idea. Last but not least, don't forget to take advantage of the networking possibilities provided by the festival— it's a terrific chance to meet other movie lovers and business people.

CHAPTER SIX

GETTING AROUND

Luxembourg is a fascinating and distinctive place to travel. This tiny nation has a lot of interesting places to explore despite its small size. You'll discover that getting around is simple and practical, whether you're looking to explore the gently rolling hills of the countryside or the busy city streets of Luxembourg City.

The train is the most widely used mode of transportation in Luxembourg. All major towns and cities in Luxembourg are connected by a sophisticated rail system. Train travel is a fantastic option because it is dependable, economical, and efficient. You can also utilize the bus system if you want to explore the countryside. Despite being slower than trains, buses can still get you where you need to go.

You can also travel by car to Luxembourg's cities and towns if you want to do so. It is simple to get about in Luxembourg because of its excellent network of roads and motorways. Also, there are several parking alternatives accessible, making it simple to locate a space for your vehicle.

Use Luxembourg's enormous network of bike routes for an even more practical mode of transportation. You can simply get from one area to another since the nation is filled with designated bike lanes. If you don't have a bike of your own, you may borrow one from a company that rents one.

Furthermore, if you want a more distinctive experience, you may tour Luxembourg by boat. You may enjoy a boat trip down the Moselle River or see Luxembourg City's canals thanks to the nation's strong maritime heritage.

You'll discover that getting about Luxembourg is simple and practical no matter which method you select. You'll discover that traveling about in Luxembourg is a fun and memorable experience, whether you're searching for a distinctive experience or just a handy method to get around.

The cost of transportation in Luxembourg varies according to the mode you choose. Using the public transportation network, which consists of buses, trains, and trams is the most cost-effective choice. The cost of a ticket varies based on the route taken and the kind of ticket purchased. For instance, a short-distance one-way ticket costs €1.20.

You may drive an automobile in Luxembourg. There are many parking alternatives accessible nationwide and gas rates are often low. There are also automobile rental firms, so if you don't have a car of your own, you may borrow one.

Lastly, you may ride a bike around Luxembourg. If you don't have a bike, you may hire one from one of the numerous cities and towns that offer bicycle rental shops. Cycling is a convenient mode of transportation, and the nation often has dedicated bike lanes.

In Luxembourg, transportation costs are often manageable. You may find a method to see the nation that matches your budget, whether you decide to drive, use public transit, or hire a bicycle.

Taxi services are available in Luxembourg if you're seeking a luxurious means of transportation. The cost of a taxi varies based on the distance, and they are readily accessible across the nation. A luxury rental agency may also be able to provide you with access to a high-end vehicle with all the bells and whistles.

Finally, you may even hire a private chauffeur if you want to travel the nation in luxury. In Luxembourg, you may hire a luxury chauffeur service to have a qualified driver transport you anywhere you need to go. If you want to travel with ease and luxury, this is a fantastic choice.

Overall, Luxembourg offers a wide range of opulent transportation choices. You may find a means to travel across the nation in luxury and elegance, whether you decide to take a cab, rent a vehicle, or hire a private driver.

I had a terrific time traveling in Luxembourg. I used the nation's public transportation system and found it to be dependable and reasonably priced. I was able to travel quickly and easily, and using the trains and buses made it simple to see the entire country. I also rented a car from a nearby business and enjoyed exploring the countryside in it. The landscape was breathtaking, and the roads were in excellent condition. Finally, I rented a bike from a local business and made use of the nation's bike paths. It was a wonderful way to see the country, and I was delighted by the clean air and breathtaking scenery. I had a good overall experience going about Luxembourg and would suggest it to others.

Make use of the public transportation network if you're trying to go about Luxembourg. It's a fantastic method to see the nation since it's safe, effective, and reasonably priced. If you want to go throughout the countryside, I would also advise hiring a vehicle since it's a convenient method to do it. Last but not least, I would also advise using the nation's bike routes and renting a bike from a local business. This is a fantastic opportunity to see the nation while also getting some exercise. In conclusion, traveling to Luxembourg is simple and convenient, and I heartily recommend it to anybody searching for a fun and distinctive experience.

PUBLIC TRANSIT

A crucial resource for its citizens and a crucial component of Luxembourg's infrastructure is public transportation. Luxembourg, one of the smallest nations in Europe with fewer than 600,000 people, is also one of the world's most densely populated nations. Public transportation plays a crucial role in connecting people to jobs, education, and other essential services in this country's densely populated areas.

Buses, trains, trams, and ferries are all part of Luxembourg's extensive public transportation system. The Société des Transports Intercommunaux (STI), which operates more than 800 buses and 88 trams, is the largest public transportation provider in the nation.

Additionally, 25 train lines run by the country's national railroad company, Chemins de Fer Luxembourgeois, link the capital city of Luxembourg City to the nearby towns.

In Luxembourg, public transportation is a convenient and economical means of transportation. The majority of Luxembourg's public transportation systems offer senior and student discounts, making it affordable and accessible to people of all ages and income levels. Additionally, using public transportation helps reduce the number of cars on the road, which lowers air pollution and carbon emissions.

The public transportation system in Luxembourg is also very secure. The nation has implemented several safety measures, including the installation of security guards, cameras, and emergency call boxes on buses and trains. Furthermore, the public transportation system in Luxembourg is well-maintained, with regular inspections and upkeep to guarantee that all vehicles are in good working order.

The use of public transportation is essential to the daily lives of the people of Luxembourg. It is a crucial component of the nation's infrastructure because it is dependable, effective, and reasonably priced. Luxembourg is well-equipped to meet the needs of its citizens, enabling them to travel safely and conveniently throughout the nation thanks to its extensive network of public transportation.

How Much Does Luxembourg Public Transportation Cost?

Depending on the kind of ticket bought, using Luxembourg's public transportation might be expensive. Chemins de Fer Luxembourgeois, the country's railroad company, provides a variety of tickets, including single, day, and monthly passes. The price of a single ticket varies from €2 to €7.50 depending on the distance. Day admissions are priced at €4.50, while monthly passes are €40.

A variety of tickets and passes, including single tickets, day tickets, and monthly passes, are available from the Société des Transports Intercommunaux (STI). Depending on the distance traveled, single tickets cost anywhere between €1 and €3. Day passes are €3, while monthly passes are €25.

Moreover, passes and tickets may be lowered for elders and students. The STI charges a senior ticket of €2 and a student ticket of €1.

In Luxembourg, using the public transit system is a quick, dependable, and secure method to travel. With a comprehensive network of buses, trains, and trams, the nation is well-linked, making it simple to get to and from any location within the nation.

The Ministry of Transport oversees the four primary modes of public transportation in Luxembourg: buses, trains, trams, and ferries. The largest transportation system is the railroad system, which includes both domestic and foreign routes. Regional railways connect the Grand

Duchy of Luxembourg's cities, while international trains link it to nations nearby including Belgium, France, and Germany.

In Luxembourg, there is a good bus system that covers the whole nation. It links to both larger cities and villages as well as smaller towns and villages, serving both urban and rural communities. The nation may be explored easily thanks to the bus network's regular operations.

While being relatively modest, Luxembourg's tram network connects several of the country's main cities. It is an easy method to get inside the city and to some of the smaller villages.

The Grand Duchy of Luxembourg and the United Kingdom are the two countries that travel by ferry the most. Traveling between these two nations and taking in the various islands in the English Channel are both made possible by this method.

Generally, using public transit to move about Luxembourg is a reliable, dependable, and safe option. With a vast network of buses, trains, trams, and ferries, the nation is well-linked, making it feasible to get anywhere in Luxembourg. Luxembourg is the perfect location for tourists searching for a simple and pleasant way to experience the nation because of its first-rate public transit system.

I can attest that Luxembourg has a first-rate public transportation system because I lived here for a while. The buses, trams, and trains are consistently dependable and on time in my experience using them. It was simple to navigate thanks to the helpful and friendly ticket office staff. I was able to travel around the region by using convenient regional and international train lines. Overall, Luxembourg's public transportation system is a reliable and secure method to travel the nation, and I heartily suggest it to anybody wishing to visit the area.

I would suggest using the public transit system if you are visiting Luxembourg for the first time. There are several transportation alternatives, including buses, trams, and trains. To plan the itinerary and make the most of your trip, I would also advise downloading an app. To navigate the city, it's also a good idea to pick up a map or guidebook. Lastly, you can always hire a bike or a scooter to tour the city at your leisure if you're feeling very daring.

TAXIS

In Luxembourg, taxi services are an essential component of the nation's transportation system, offering dependable and practical transportation for both locals and visitors. Getting about Luxembourg is a snap because of its highly effective taxi fleet, simple booking processes, and affordable prices.

A variety of businesses, from big, global ones like TAXI Luxembourg to smaller, regional ones, provide taxi services in Luxembourg. No of the size of the business, all cabs are kept in excellent condition, and all of the drivers are very skilled and informed. All taxi drivers are needed to be licensed, have a current driver's license, and have a thorough understanding of the local area.

In Luxembourg, there are a few considerations to make while ordering a cab. To guarantee you obtain the greatest bargain, it's crucial to check pricing amongst various businesses beforehand. It's also essential to inquire about the kind of car offered and the maximum quantity of baggage it can hold. Also, certain businesses could provide discounted pricing for particular locations or times of the day.

The majority of taxi firms in Luxembourg have online booking options, as well as phone and app-based booking services, making the cab booking procedure quite simple. Also, a lot of taxi services provide a selection of payment choices, such as cash, credit cards, and even PayPal.

The country's taxis provide a simple and effective means of transportation. The nation's taxi services make traveling about a snap with their highly qualified drivers, affordable prices, and simple booking choices. The taxi services in Luxembourg are certain to provide you with a dependable and pleasurable experience whether you're a commuter, a tourist, or just in need of a ride.

The distance and vehicle type you choose will affect the price of a taxi in Luxembourg. Prices typically start at around €2.50 per kilometer, including waiting hours and baggage fees. The time of day may also affect prices, with peak hours requiring greater fees. It's advisable to get in touch with a nearby taxi company immediately for a more accurate price.

In Luxembourg, my experience using cabs has been extraordinarily pleasant. The cars are cozy and well-kept, the drivers are always kind and competent, and the charges are often extremely reasonable. With the majority of businesses providing online, phone, and app-based booking systems, hiring a cab is also quite simple. Overall, I feel that using a cab in Luxembourg is a quick and simple method to move about.

The easiest approach to guarantee you receive the greatest bargain while using cabs in Luxembourg is to constantly make sure to check pricing across various firms. Asking about the kind of car available and how much baggage it can hold is also vital. To assure availability and the cheapest price, always reserve a cab in advance.

CHAPTER SEVEN

THE DOS AND DONTS OF A TOURIST

Going to a new nation may be an exciting and unique experience, but it can also be stressful if you are unfamiliar with the dos and don'ts of that country. This is particularly true while traveling to Luxembourg, a tiny European nation noted for its ancient landmarks, lively culture, and one-of-a-kind attractions. As a visitor to Luxembourg, it is essential to learn the country's traditions and etiquette to have the most pleasurable and stress-free visit possible.

These are some dos and don'ts to remember while visiting Luxembourg:

DO:

- Be mindful of the local culture and traditions. Although a modern and advanced nation, Luxembourg has its own set of social practices and cultural standards. Before visiting, learn about the country's etiquette and traditions, and treat natives with respect and civility.

- Learn a little bit of the local language. Luxembourgish is the official language of Luxembourg, and the majority of the population speaks it. Learning a few fundamental words in Luxembourgish can make your stay much more pleasurable.

- Take advantage of the outdoor attractions of Luxembourg. Hiking, motorcycling, and kayaking are just a few of the outdoor activities available in Luxembourg. Take some time to discover the natural and scenic beauties of the land.

DON'T:

- Avoid being too loud or obnoxious in public areas. Luxembourg is a tiny nation, so it's crucial to be aware of your surroundings and have a courteous demeanor while you're out and about.

- Remember to dress correctly. Since Luxembourg is a conservative nation, dress modestly and politely while out in public.

• Don't forget to plan ahead of time. Luxembourg is a tiny nation, and getting about without a plan might be challenging. Before you go, do some research about the nation and plan out what you want to do and see.

Overall, Luxembourg is a lovely and interesting place to visit, and following these dos and don'ts will make your vacation as joyful and stress-free as possible. Thus, spend a few minutes researching the nation and planning your vacation, and you'll have an outstanding time in Luxembourg.

My time in Luxembourg was very good. I relocated to Luxembourg from the United States for employment and ended up staying for two incredible years. I was lured to Luxembourg because of offers excellent work possibilities and a robust economy. With its gorgeous scenery, wonderful cuisine, and nice people, Luxembourg rapidly became a terrific location to live for me.

Luxembourg's folks were among the friendliest and most welcome I'd ever met. Everyone was pleasant and honest, and they made me feel at ease. I got the chance to travel across the nation, learn about the culture, and try new things. I was able to mingle with the people and learn the language.

Overall, my time in Luxembourg was really good, and I would strongly suggest it to anybody wishing to immerse themselves in a new culture.

The nation has a lot to offer and is a wonderful location to live, work, and explore.

HEALTHY AND SAFETY TIPS

To guarantee a safe and pleasurable journey as a tourist in Luxembourg, it is essential to keep a healthy lifestyle and practice safety. Here are some pointers to keep you safe and healthy when visiting Luxembourg.

1. Understand Local Laws: Understanding the rules of the nation you are visiting might help you be safe and healthy while in Luxembourg. Before your journey, be sure to investigate the local laws and traditions. This may help you avoid any legal difficulties or other safety concerns.

2. Be Hydrated: While visiting Luxembourg, it is essential to drink lots of water. While the average temperature in Luxembourg is approximately 65°F (18°C), keeping hydrated is critical. Bring a water bottle with you and refill it periodically with clean, safe drinking water.

3. Bring Comfortable Shoes: Luxembourg is a wonderful nation with many amazing sights to see. Use comfy shoes to guarantee that you can do so without pain. This will assist to avoid foot and ankle ailments and make your journey more pleasurable.

4. Use sunscreen: Since the sun may be harsh in Luxembourg, it is essential to protect your skin from the sun's damaging rays. Bring high-quality sunscreen with you and reapply it often throughout the day. This will help you avoid sunburn and other skin damage.

5. Practice Food Safety: Luxembourg boasts a diverse range of delectable foods. While dining in Luxembourg, however, it is essential to exercise food safety. Be careful to only consume properly prepared food and to avoid anything that looks or smells suspect.

Here are just a few pointers to keep you safe and healthy while visiting Luxembourg. By following these guidelines, you may guarantee that your vacation to Luxembourg is both safe and pleasant

There are several rules and regulations in Luxembourg that tourists should be aware of before going. In terms of public conduct, Luxembourg has laws prohibiting public intoxication, drug usage, and public nudity. Also, smoking is prohibited in many public spaces in Luxembourg, so be sure to check local signs before lighting up.

Additional laws to be aware of concern public transportation. All public transportation services in Luxembourg need a valid ticket to travel. It is also prohibited to blast loud music or otherwise disrupt public transit.

Thankfully, Luxembourg has some photography laws. Photographers should be aware that photographing military sites, government buildings, and any other areas designated sensitive by the government is forbidden. Visitors should also always obtain permission before photographing someone.

Visitors may guarantee a safe and pleasurable journey to Luxembourg by being familiar with the local rules and regulations.

I just went on vacation to Luxembourg and found it to be a safe and delightful destination to visit. I followed the advice above to keep healthy and safe during my vacation. When traveling the nation, I made care to remain hydrated, wear comfortable shoes, and practice excellent food safety. I also examined local laws and regulations to verify that I was abiding by all of them.

Overall, I had a nice time in Luxembourg. During my journey, I felt secure and comfortable, and I had a terrific time visiting the nation. I would strongly suggest Luxembourg as a vacation location.

My recommendation to travelers visiting Luxembourg is to learn about the country's rules and regulations. This will assist guarantee that you obey all of the laws and regulations when traveling across the nation. When in Luxembourg, remember to remain hydrated, wear comfortable shoes, and practice food safety. Lastly, when traveling, be alert to your surroundings and use common sense to protect yourself and others. Following these recommendations can help you have a safe and happy vacation in Luxembourg.

GENERAL TIPS

Going to Luxembourg may be an exciting experience, but it's vital to be prepared and to know what you're getting into. Here are a few basic recommendations that will help you make the most of your vacation to Luxembourg.

1. Research Before You Go. Before your travel, study the traditions and culture of Luxembourg, including the dos and don'ts of local etiquette. This will allow you to avoid any cultural faux pas throughout your visit.

2. Have Your Documents Ready. Be sure that you have all of the essential documentation for admission into Luxembourg, including your passport and visa if applicable.

3. Prepare for the Weather. Luxembourg's temperature may be unpredictable, so it's vital to prepare for both warm and cold weather. Bring layers of clothes and rain gear, since you may need them.

4. Respect Local Laws. Be informed of and observe the laws of Luxembourg. This will assist to guarantee that your stay is comfortable and free of any legal issues.

5. Be Careful While Utilizing Public Transportation. Public transit in Luxembourg may be hectic, so it's necessary to be careful while utilizing it. Be mindful of your possessions and look out for pickpockets.

6. Use Cash. Credit cards are accepted in many locations in Luxembourg, but it's essential to keep some cash on hand for minor purchases and in case of an emergency.

7. Take Care While Driving. The roads in Luxembourg may be complicated and hazardous, so it's necessary to drive cautiously and defensively. Be informed of the local norms of the road and be prepared for unforeseen challenges.

8. Be Safe. Luxembourg is typically a safe location, however, practice common prudence while touring the city. Be cautious of your surroundings, remain in well-lit locations, and leave your valuables at home.

Following these easy guidelines might assist you to make the most of your vacation to Luxembourg. By being prepared and educated, you can guarantee that your stay is pleasurable and safe.

CONSIDERABLE SAVING TIPS

Saving money is an essential part of financial planning and a key factor in securing a financially sound future. Unfortunately, saving money can be difficult in today's fast-paced society where spending is often seen as essential and saving is seen as a waste of time.

However, several saving tips can help you build up your savings over time. By following these tips, you can begin to save more and find ways to make your money work for you.

1. Track Your Expenses: Tracking your expenses is one of the most important tips for saving money. Take a look at your spending habits and make a budget. This can help you find places where you can save. Look for areas in which you may make savings, including superfluous spending and luxury things.

2. Create a Savings Plan: After you have identified places where you can save, make a plan of action. Establish a target of how much you want to save each month and stick to it. Automating your savings might also help you remain on target.

3. Take Use of Discounts: There are various discounts accessible in today's industry. Take advantage of any discounts or promo codes that you come across. You may also join loyalty programs or utilize cashback apps to save money on purchases.

4. Seek for Alternatives: Instead of purchasing anything new, search for alternatives. For example, try to borrow products from friends or family rather than purchasing them. You may also attempt to locate secondhand products or buy at thrift shops to save money.

5. Adhere to Your Budget: After you have established a budget, keep to it. Be sure you pay yourself first by designating a specific amount of money each month to your savings. This should be done before you pay your bills or purchase anything else.

By following these strategies, you may begin to save more and develop large savings. Saving money is an essential aspect of financial planning and a significant factor in establishing a good financial future. By recording your costs, developing a savings plan, taking advantage of discounts, exploring alternatives, and keeping to your budget, you may begin to save more and create large savings.

I have been using the savings ideas I outlined above for my budget and have found them to be quite useful. By analyzing my costs, developing a savings plan, taking advantage of discounts, and searching for alternatives, I have been able to save a large amount of money each month. I have also found that sticking to my budget has been essential for me to stay on track and reach my goals. Overall, I am very happy with the results that I have seen and will continue to apply these tips to my finances.

If you are a first-timer trying to save money, my advice would be to start by tracking your expenses and making a budget. This will help you identify areas where you can make cuts and find ways to save money. Additionally, take advantage of discounts, look for alternatives, and stick to your budget. By following these strategies, you may begin to save more and develop large savings. Lastly, don't forget to pay yourself first by designating a specific amount of money each month to your savings. This will help you attain your objectives and guarantee a financially stable future.

CHAPTER EIGHT
RESOURCES

Luxembourg is a tiny yet strong nation in central Europe. It has a lot to offer both tourists and locals, from beautiful scenery and historical sites to vibrant culture and delectable cuisine. In addition to these, Luxembourg has several resources available to help you make the most of your stay. Below are some of the most essential tourism resources in Luxembourg.

Luxembourg Tourist Board: The official Luxembourg Tourism website is the best place to begin planning your trip. It contains all of the necessary information about the country, including detailed descriptions of attractions, activities, and events, as well as helpful tips and advice.

The Luxembourg City Card is an excellent resource if you intend to stay in Luxembourg for more than one day. It provides free or reduced admission to many tourist attractions, museums, parks, and public transportation.

Luxembourg Tourist Guide: The official tourist guide of Luxembourg is an excellent resource for learning about the country's history and culture. It's also jam-packed with useful tips and advice, covering everything from the best restaurants and shopping spots to the best places to stay.

The Luxembourg Tourist Office is the official website of the Luxembourg Tourism Board, and it provides detailed information about the country, its attractions, activities, events, and more. It's an excellent resource for detailed information about the country and its many attractions.

Luxembourg Public Transportation: Luxembourg has excellent public transportation that makes getting around the country simple. The Luxembourg Transport Guide provides detailed information on various modes of transportation, such as trains, buses, trams, and more.

Luxembourg Travel Guide Books: There are many travel guidebooks available if you want more detailed information about Luxembourg. These publications contain thorough information about the nation, its history, culture, and attractions, as well as practical travel suggestions.

Luxembourg Mobile App: Luxembourg provides a mobile app that is a useful resource for trip preparation. The app provides thorough information on sights, activities, and events, as well as helpful hints and ideas. You may also learn about the newest news, events, and promotions, as well as buy attraction tickets.

I recently had the chance to visit Luxembourg and was able to make the most of my time there by taking use of the various resources available. I began my study by visiting the official

Luxembourg Tourism website, which gave me a thorough grasp of the country's attractions and activities. The Luxembourg mobile app was subsequently downloaded on my smartphone, which kept me up to speed on the latest news and offers.

When I first came to Luxembourg, I used the Luxembourg City Card, which provided me with free or subsidized access to attractions and public transit. I also purchased a copy of the official tourist guide, which contained detailed information about the country, its history, and culture, as well as practical advice for making the most of my time there.

During my visit, I explored the country and learned about its culture by visiting the many attractions, participating in local events, exploring the countryside, and sampling the delectable cuisine. I also had the opportunity to see various historical places, including the Grand Ducal Palace and the City of Luxembourg.

Overall, owing to the tools offered, I had a fantastic time in Luxembourg. I was able to make the most of my stay and explore the country by using the official website, mobile app, and tourist guide.

As a first-time visitor to Luxembourg, I recommend that you take advantage of all available resources to make the most of your stay.

Begin by conducting research online, such as on the official Luxembourg Tourism website, to gain an understanding of the country's attractions and activities. Consider downloading the Luxembourg mobile app on your smartphone to keep up with the latest news and deals.

When you arrive in Luxembourg, make use of the various resources available, such as the Luxembourg City Card, which provides free or subsidized admission to attractions and public transit. Pick up a copy of the official tourist guide, which will provide you with detailed information about the country, its history, and culture, as well as practical advice on how to make the most of your time there.

Lastly, remember to tour the nation and immerse yourself in its culture. Visit the many attractions, participate in local events, explore the countryside, and sample the delectable cuisine. Luxembourg is a small but powerful country with many attractions. Enjoy!

FUN FACTS ABOUT LUXEMBOURG

Luxembourg is a tiny country in central Europe that is an important participant in the European Union and a famous tourist destination. It has a rich culture and history, and tourists may experience the country's various attractions. Here are some interesting Luxembourg facts that you may not know.

1. Luxembourg is the only Grand Duchy in the world. The Grand Duchy of Luxembourg is ruled by a monarch, who is now Grand Duke Henri of Luxembourg. The nation is the world's only grand duchy, and its grand duke is the world's only surviving grand duke.

2. Luxembourg is one of the tiniest nations in the world. It is one of the world's tiniest nations, with a land area of just 2,586 square kilometers.

3. The world's oldest restaurant is located in Luxembourg. The Auberge de la Petite Cour is a restaurant that was founded in 1728 and is still in business today.

4. Luxembourg is a multilingual nation. German, French, and Luxembourgish are the official languages, however, English is commonly spoken.

5. Since 1957, Luxembourg has been a member of the European Union. The nation is a founder member of the European Union, having joined in 1957.

6. Luxembourg is home to the only American-style theme park in Europe. "Little Europe," a Luxembourgish theme park, contains rides, attractions, and games from all around Europe.

7. Luxembourg has a diverse cultural heritage. Several museums, castles, cathedrals, and other historical monuments in the nation are designated as UNESCO World Heritage Sites.

8. Luxembourg is the world's second wealthiest nation. According to the World Bank, Luxembourg has the world's second-highest GDP per capita, after only Qatar.

9. Luxembourg is one of Europe's greenest nations. The nation has several parks and woods, and its forests encompass more than a third of the entire land area.

10. The world's only subterranean brewery is located in Luxembourg. The Caves of St. Martin brewery is housed in a series of caverns built into the rocks near Vianden. Guests may visit the caverns and drink the beers made there.

11. Luxembourg has the world's highest rate of internet use. Eurostat reports that the nation has a 100% internet penetration rate.

12. In Luxembourg, the first European Union-wide visa for non-EU passengers was issued.

13. Luxembourg is one of Europe's most cosmopolitan nations. The nation is home to individuals from more than 170 different countries, according to the World Bank.

14. Luxembourg is routinely ranked as one of the world's safest nations. According to the World Peace Index, the nation ranks fourth in the world in terms of safety.

15. Luxembourg has Europe's first public radio station. Radio Luxembourg started transmitting in 1929 and is still the country's oldest radio station today.

Here are just a few interesting Luxembourg facts.

SUMMARY

Luxembourg, with its scenic scenery, lively towns, and rich cultural legacy, is one of the most attractive nations in the world. This travel book provides a thorough summary of all the incredible sights that this small nation has to offer. This book offers an in-depth look into the heart and spirit of Luxembourg, from its magnificent palaces and historical monuments to its intriguing museums, outdoor activities, and delectable food. This book has something for everyone, whether you want a thrilling journey, a peaceful vacation, or a cultural experience. Uncover the best that Luxemburg has to offer and begin arranging your ideal trip today.

Printed in Great Britain
by Amazon